Software Testing for Managers

An Introduction to Strategies, Technologies, and Best Practices

Ross Radford

Apress®

Software Testing for Managers: An Introduction to Strategies, Technologies, and Best Practices

Ross Radford
Elgin, TX, USA

ISBN-13 (pbk): 979-8-8688-0571-4　　　　　　ISBN-13 (electronic): 979-8-8688-0572-1
https://doi.org/10.1007/979-8-8688-0572-1

Copyright © 2024 by Ross Radford

Managing Director, Apress Media LLC: Welmoed Spahr
Acquisitions Editor: Susan McDermott
Development Editor: Laura Berendson
Project Manager: Jessica Vakili

Distributed to the book trade worldwide by Springer Science+Business Media New York, 1 NY Plaza, New York, NY 10004. Phone 1-800-SPRINGER, fax (201) 348-4505, e-mail orders-ny@ springer-sbm.com, or visit www.springeronline.com. Apress Media, LLC is a California LLC and the sole member (owner) is Springer Science + Business Media Finance Inc (SSBM Finance Inc). SSBM Finance Inc is a **Delaware** corporation.

For information on translations, please e-mail booktranslations@springernature.com; for reprint, paperback, or audio rights, please e-mail bookpermissions@springernature.com.

Apress titles may be purchased in bulk for academic, corporate, or promotional use. eBook versions and licenses are also available for most titles. For more information, reference our Print and eBook Bulk Sales web page at http://www.apress.com/bulk-sales.

Any source code or other supplementary material referenced by the author in this book is available to readers on the Github repository: https://github.com/Apress/Software-Testing-For-Managers. For more detailed information, please visit https://www.apress.com/gp/services/source-code.

If disposing of this product, please recycle the paper

Table of Contents

About the Author

Ross Radford is the founder of testfromthetop.com and is on a mission to bring test awareness to leadership. He has spent a career developing and testing enterprise-level software for huge projects serving millions of users. He knows leaders are in a unique position to unblock and prioritize quality assurance at every level. Radford developed knowledge sharing presentations for peers, online courses and conference talks, with the common feedback from software engineers: "This is great. Now convince my boss!" He set out to do just that.

About the Technical Reviewer

Kelly I. Hitchcock graduated from Missouri State University with what her parents called a useless BA in creative writing. She leveraged that useless degree into a 10-year technical writing career and then another 10 years (and counting!) in quality assurance. She derives an unhealthy amount of satisfaction from a well-written test plan and working, human-readable test automation. In the spare time she desperately lacks, Kelly writes fiction and picks up the LEGO bricks her kids can't see.

Introduction

My name is Ross Radford, and I love software testing. Weird but true!

I've spent my whole career, first as a software engineer and later as a manager, testing software. Let me back up a bit; I wasn't always focused exclusively on testing. I spent a decade building enterprise-level software for millions of users at one of the largest financial technology companies in the world, Experian. That's the credit bureau. Not the one that had the nasty data breach—you're thinking of the other one with a similar name. At least as of the writing of this book.

Writing software is all about bugs. Other people's bugs, of course, since your code always works. Just kidding. If you write code, you write bugs. We can boil it down even more:

Code = bugs.

Wait, that's an assignment operation. A bug in logic.

Code == bugs;

Always, all code. Yes, even that code, yes really. As a coder, you can only see so many bugs made by yourself and others before you start to wonder about the imperfect nature of human creative experience. Existential crisis perhaps, or Buddhist-style acceptance that life is suffering. Or maybe you start looking into testing. That's what I did.

I'm going to bare my soul a little and admit I'm not a great coder. Above-average at best. I make up for it with my extreme versatility, intrepid attitude, and ability to quickly learn and adapt.

Okay no, that's bullshit. I'll try again. I make up for my average coding skills with methodical adherence to process. Yep, that's closer to true.

Project management made my life easier as an engineer. Less vagary around expectations means less guesswork and misunderstanding. Properly using tools like version control, not to mention using it the right way when collaborating with a large team, is the difference between hair-on-fire catastrophe and an uneventful professional routine.

Testing gives an engineer invaluable confidence. A reliable check against common bugs *before* anyone else sees your work. For a shy junior coder, this is a revelation.

Another reason I'm an okay-coder (last one, promise) is my natural curiosity. If there's a "correct" or "best" or just "better" way to do something, I'll try it out. So, once I felt like I was hitting a ceiling for skills developing enterprise web applications, I jumped deep into automated testing.

Now, if you're picturing me in a software job just running whole-hog into a niche technology without blessing from management, let me assure you it wasn't that easy. Buy-in from test-aware leadership is absolutely crucial. I'm fortunate my boss (and their boss, and their boss's boss) received a mandate for better quality and less bugs in production. Boom, there was my business case.

Testing is great, but it's not just a technical effort, it's an organization-level concern. The entire company, yes. Chapter 1 - Test Awareness will make it obvious why. I've read every book I could find on software management and testing. There's a glut of books about unit testing or the latest techniques to test software on a code level, but not many on how management facilitates testing, when that is absolutely key to setting your team up for success.

It's a real problem! I've given presentations on software testing at conferences. I would get excited about a new concept or technology and carefully prepare a guide for my peers to get started with this new software testing panacea I think will help. I speak my mind and the audience applauds. Or not, depending on how late in the day and the conference catering situation. Maybe someone got something out of my talk, hopefully. I've heard the feedback many times from engineers though: "This is great; good idea. Now convince my boss!"

I've interviewed friends in the spirit of "What do you wish your boss knew about testing?" I tried to get the most candid answer possible, all to make the point that leadership has to *lead* testing efforts.

This book is about testing software from a high-level perspective. We will avoid venturing into the wilderness of technical detail, because it piles up fast and can be a major distraction.

I'll explain just what I mean by that: in Chapter 1, we contrast the perspectives of individual team members against the leader owning and overseeing the whole process. Closer to the code, an individual engineer simply can't have the full view of what is needed to build testing practice into every level of the software development lifecycle. They might only see a green check mark on their unit tests and call it a day. Granted, many can see the bigger picture, but still they are not empowered to set policy.

Policy and process is *our* job.[1]

My goal is to present high-level information that is concise, comprehensible, and actionable immediately.

I'll try not to bury you in technical jargon. There will be some esoteric terminology occasionally. There's a glossary in the back when you need it.

We will refer to the software development lifecycle frequently. I assume you are aware of this concept if not intimately familiar. Not necessarily in the sense of an Agile workflow, but the larger idea of a pipeline from idea to product.

I'm also going to skip making the case for testing. If you're reading this, you probably have a mandated testing requirement or pressure to improve quality, or maybe you simply want to produce better software for less time and effort. Whatever your reason, I'm glad we met.

Thank you for taking an interest in testing. For me, it's personal.

---

[1] If you're an engineer or other individual contributor: First of all, thank you for buying this book, and I hope you like it. Please give a copy to your boss!

CHAPTER 1

Test Awareness

You are already testing, if you realize it or not.

Let's tell the tale of new code. A familiar story we all know and love. Perhaps your parents read this one to you as a young child. Did I mention my mother is an executive project manager? She is.

So let's follow along and observe a new piece of code from inception and planning to the final pushout of the nest and into the world.

First, planning. Stakeholders will specify the new work. It might be a formal specification document, a list of acceptance criteria, or an informal order such as a bug fix ("It's broke. Fix it!"). A project manager will likely help track the new work and, together with the engineer assigned the task, come up with a reasonable estimate for the time required to finish. Expectations set, it's time to start coding.

Software engineers test iteratively every step while developing their work.

A senior engineer will review a peer's work, either looking at code directly or asking for a quick demonstration, or both.

Once the work is done and integrated with the main application, a QA team may take a look at it. A quality assurance engineer or team will run a version of the application in a safe, simulated environment away from public view. They will figure out what part of the system this new code affects, document a test plan, access that subsystem, try to use it, and record the results.

© Ross Radford 2024
R. Radford, *Software Testing for Managers*, https://doi.org/10.1007/979-8-8688-0572-1_1

This is the point in the story where most teams implement automated testing.

For this story, let's skip that (important) step and come back to it.

Let's say everything seems to function as it should.

Now, other stakeholders need to review the new work. A product representative may request a live demo before they sign off on a bug fix or new feature. A customer waiting for the work may want a demonstration or even to review the code depending on the terms of their business relationship.

Security auditing, regulatory compliance, accessibility—there are many possible stakeholders who may require a review before the new work is accepted.

Your final frontier is your user. Whatever the review process, the final test is in the hands of actual users in the real world. Users are known for using software in unpredictable ways: even with the best of intentions, they will find bugs, if bugs exist. Sometimes users don't have the best intentions and will patiently test our software for security holes or embarrassing design flaws. They might even loudly give feedback on public social media. Thanks users, super helpful!

Now that our new code has made it through the software development lifecycle, where was the testing? Recall we skipped mention of automated testing in our account.

Omitting automated testing for this example focuses our attention on the "manual" testing that happens at every step of our development lifecycle, from the start of development to the final review. This process *works*. Many organizations ship quality code this way, without extensive automated testing. If your personal situation looks similar to the example, that's just fine. If you have a working process delivering results, great! It only gets better from here.

Everyone involved tested the software, whether they realized it or not. At every stage, testing can also be automated. Yet, just because we can, doesn't mean we should. We'll get into where and when to automate testing in the next chapter.

Let's realize and appreciate the fact that testing happens continuously across the software development lifecycle.

Next, let's talk about an individual contributor and how their perspective differs from yours—the leader.

1.1 The Software Engineer

As mentioned in the story, the most obvious place for a big testing effort is after development, but before release to production.

Directly after development work is done, your new code will get *reintegrated* to the main application, snapping into place and hopefully not breaking anything in the process. This process breaks often. Because of the risk, this is a good place for an automated testing suite to run and either pass or defenestrate your new code before it has a chance to do any real-world damage. Those tests are a kind of robot gatekeeper.

You might realize the savvy software engineer can save time by running those same gatekeeper tests themselves locally on their own machine before attempting to reintegrate the code. Indeed, long before that, even before the code is done, tests can be run continually during development.

To a software engineer, testing appears to happen most critically during reintegration, after their new work is complete. An engineer understands that code frequently comes back with bugs, and as the original writer, they will likely have to fix it. For a meticulous engineer, testing reduces the risk of bug fixes, so they will test early and often. For a more cynical-minded engineer, the gatekeeper test suite prevents co-workers from unintentionally breaking everything with their buggy code. Despite the benefits, busy coders sometimes grumble about adding more development time to actually write the tests. Often, testing can be a sidebar for work estimates, tacked on at the last minute. Testing can seem like tedious extra work of inquantifiable value, like writing documentation or time tracking. Often, engineers are under time pressure to provide a bug fix or emergency new code as soon as possible. Testing can easily get overlooked.

As a leader, you are in a unique position to address that friction, by setting test writing time for your engineers as a priority or even requirement when delivering new code. The downside to a unilateral policy on test writing can be ineffective, low-value tests bulking up your test suites. Signaling to your engineers that they only need to focus on testing when testing is truly valuable can mitigate the malaise that builds up with mandated test writing.

Planning

Director
- Sets the priority for testing, unlocking the ability to schedule time in project estimates.

Software Engineer
- Considers testing as part of the development plan, which may have significant impact on time estimates.

Development

Director
- Works to facilitate test resources are available as early in development as possible. Collaborates with Senior Engineers to set best practices for testing during development and code review.

Software Engineer

- Writes application code. Either writes test code during or after development, or if adequate coverage already exists, not at all.

Internal Staging

Director
- Oversee QA process, ensure high-value tests are run. Decide what level of test coverage is essential.

Software Engineer

- Helps QA run tests for their specific code.
- Responds to bug reports.

External Staging

Director
- Communicate progress with stakeholders. Share testing resources if possible. Supervise demo presentations. Supervise User Acceptance Testing and communicate results.

Software Engineer

- Prepare code demonstrations.
- Respond to bug reports.

Production

Director
- Continually monitor for user feedback and production bugs.

Software Engineer
- Respond to bug reports
- support emergency patch efforts.

I'm making this comparison to show how testing is facilitated at the top level of any organization and just as easily it can be neglected. Testing from the top-down unlocks the potential for world-class quality assurance. Individual contributors, QA engineers, project managers, even team leads can't do it alone!

The point I want you to consider is that while you as a leader have the most influence on testing and culture at your organization, every member of your team should have the *awareness* of testing and where it fits in the development lifecycle. Test awareness should inform all your hiring decisions.

1.2 Summary

- Testing happens to all software, intentionally or not. Be intentional about it.

- Manual testing happens naturally every step of the software development lifecycle and can be automated at each.

- Leaders facilitate testing by allocating time and contributing to a culture that values tests.

- Every member of your team should have the *awareness* of testing and where it fits in the development lifecycle.

- Test awareness should inform all your hiring decisions.

CHAPTER 2

Test-Driven Development vs. Test During Development

This chapter examines testing opportunities along each step in the development process, with practical consideration for when to expend time and effort and when to hold back.

2.1 Testing Dogma vs. Practicality

Test-driven development is a technique where a test is written first and the code to make it work is added until the test passes. This method is part of a movement called extreme programming, invented in the 1990s as part of the extreme sports movement popularized by MTV.

Questionable origins aside, test-driven development is considered an ideal software method by some engineers. That's only part of the story though—of course not everyone agrees. That disparity is what I want to highlight here, because there are many such idealized concepts in testing that just don't gibe with practical reality.

Test-driven development as a term gives the impression it would pertain to just about all aspects of software, but that's not the case, TDD is generally only applicable to unit testing, that is, automated tests on

© Ross Radford 2024
R. Radford, *Software Testing for Managers*, https://doi.org/10.1007/979-8-8688-0572-1_2

the lowest level of code. Higher-level tests like user interface interaction or security testing are not included. TDD is specific to a kind of testing only software engineers can truly leverage, as opposed to a less technical quality assurance or user acceptance testing engineer.

Ask three random software engineers about test-driven development, and you'll get three wildly different opinions, but most generally settle with a resigned "It's great if you know what you're doing." And that, dear manager, is the issue. Requisite expertise for effective TDD is actually somewhat rare in the industry. The learning curve is steep, and most engineers simply don't love writing tests, let alone starting with tests before getting to the primary work. For that reason, TDD is a senior-level skill, advanced enough to be uncommon.

I hope it's obvious that a managerial policy dictating test-driven development is going to require either hiring only the most senior coders or an education effort throughout your development team with coaching and mentoring, likely hampering productivity until everyone is brought up to speed. For these reasons alone, I can't recommend chasing down the ideal of test-driven development. Are your engineering teams even writing tests regularly? Get there first. How's your backlog of tests that need repair? Are we sure we want to write unit tests for every new line of code, no matter what? If you're like most organizations, the answer is *probably not*.

Let's not try to run before we can walk.

To get the most value out of testing, the key question is: Are your existing tests being run consistently?

Before we can worry about test-*driven* development, let's try to test *during* development.

"Development" as in the software development lifecycle refers to every step in the process as software is built, a big moving target. "Development" also refers to the specific phase of the cycle where software engineers write code.

Software Development Lifecycle

Planning ⇨ Development ⇨ Staging Internal ⇨ Staging External ⇨ Production

I hope this looks like a simplified representation, because it is. The basic phases are in place, and I split out staging into two parts, a common pattern. Your process could be different and probably is. At any point, the horizontal steps in the diagram could easily fan out into distinct *environments*.

An environment is where your software runs. Like a majestic elk running around a mountain field, consuming resources and interacting with other flora and fauna around them. Maybe not an apt metaphor, let's get more specific. The production phase, for example, may be where our example software application lives on a publicly available server. These days, public access is likely spread across several distributed cloud computing locations or regions. Your staging phase might be segmented into different servers for multiple teams within your team, and so on. Your process diagram will likely look more like a tree with several branches or a stack of cards at every phase showing different environments. Hopefully not a fragile house of cards.

For our discussion, I collapsed it down, but you certainly will need to know all about your organization's environment collection. (Or biome? Never mind.)

I'm keeping the lifecycle relatively simple because there's another layer of complexity we have to consider: version control. For each environment your software lives in, the version of your application must also be tracked.

Tests you run against your application at any phase of the lifecycle will be run on a specific version of that application, in a specific environment.

Software Development Lifecycle
With Version per Stage

Planning	⇨	Development	⇨	Staging Internal	⇨	Staging External	⇨	Production
v2.2.0		v2.2.0		v2.1.5		v2.1.0		v1.9.0

Your application moving through the lifecycle is quite literally a moving target.

When version 1.0 is in production, version 3.0 is in development, and 2.0 is on external staging, also remember that each phase represents testing and review work that will result in more changes for each of those versions. Version 1.0 will change significantly before it reaches production, and by then, version 2.0 might be chugging along in staging, itself changing quite a bit from where it began. All the new work in 1.0 that makes it production-ready needs to be added back into 2.0. The best way to handle that is to freeze new code work on 1.0 as it gets pushed out of the nest and flies gloriously into public view. Even with a code freeze, astute readers will know bugs are reported on our version 1.0 in production, and those will have to be mixed back into later versions.

Version control is an important part of all software development, especially testing. Proper version control practices are the difference between success and repeated, punishing, morale-destroying failure. I'm going to call version control out as a concern where appropriate and tie it back into the discussion wherever I can. I'm a firm believer that any versioning tools are better than none, so whatever you're working with, every member of your development team should meet a basic proficiency and demonstrate consistent use. Semantic versioning systems ensure a sane schema for all those wild version numbers. It can be a bit of an art, but once you stick to a plan, some long string of numbers like "1.0.8.4.6.10_a" can tell you a huge amount of relevant detail about that particular version.

Now, picture testing your software in every version AND phase of the lifecycle. Every time a version is undergoing testing, we need to keep a record of the results and environment it tested in. These data are used to estimate *test coverage*, a deep topic we will explore in Chapter 6.

You can see that your perspective of the total process from a high level is critical to making decisions as a leader. Tracking progress through the lifecycle is a serious undertaking. Great project managers are your best asset here, and they need to know about testing, too. Everyone involved should be test-aware.

Let's examine the opportunities for testing at every phase of the software development lifecycle.

2.2 Specification

Chapter 4 is dedicated to specification—it's that important. You're likely working with some kind of specification already, even if it's not formalized. If you have a formal process, good!

Sometimes, developers know specifications as technical documents only, such as the specification of an application programming interface, a very literal list of rules to be followed. These are important, of course, but too many teams neglect to formalize their day-to-day workflow with specifications.

The main benefit of writing specifications for work is clarity along the process. You absolutely need to involve your client or whoever is asking for the work. Get them in the room. You want your client/customer/boss to agree with your engineers, QA testers, and project managers. Set your expectations for timelines, quality standards, how it should look when it's working, and what shade of bright red the error message font will be when something breaks.

The specifications can become your tests. When you define the spec, you define the expected behavior of the system. When the system is undergoing tests, there may be unspecified behavior, this is an error or a bug. An occasionally entertaining twist is when an unspecified behavior is a valid scenario that you forgot to add to the specification, hilarity ensues.

Specifications can become a single, shared source of truth for system behavior, usable and reliable even after they are implemented in the actual system.

The specification phase is extremely important to all your testing, and it's worth bringing in your best senior software and quality assurance engineers to collaborate and help write the specification alongside your client or product team. Even a brief sanity check–focused discussion is incredibly valuable at this stage, since missing pieces here will echo out through the rest of the work as it's completed. Errors and omissions will cause confusion at best, missed deadlines and expensive rework at some indeterminate point in the future at worst. Don't worry, we'll dig in more in Chapter 4.

Specification is clearly critical for test planning. It may seem there's not much use for actual testing at this phase, but consider the most typical scenario: Adding new code to extend some existing functionality.

The engineer conscripted into helping you plan the new work is likely pretty knowledgeable about the system and can usually tell you right off the top of their head what needs to be done, what parts of the system will need changes, and which others may be affected. However, no one individual can fully understand every aspect of most modern systems— they're just too complex. The answer may be some investigative research. This investigation will involve examining the code and reasoning about its behavior, but a much more reliable way to investigate a new system use case is to test it directly, actually running the code. A flexible automated testing system helps here, able to adjust variables and inputs to as-yet unknown settings. This is a great example of test code reuse, which we will cover in depth in Chapter 6.

There is another way your software engineers at every level can make better decisions, and that is enlisting the help of the business domain experts. This is someone who knows the product inside and out, common use cases, and limitations.

Such as "No, a registered user must be a real adult human with a social security number, no mythical animals allowed."

Boom! Just that quick conversation tells you that your carefully designed specification to register mermaids into your car insurance mobile application simply isn't going to work without extensive redesign, and probably a database schema update.

The domain expert could be a product representative, but in my experience, a large product team tends to segment talent into specialized experts who may not have the full picture of every feature. My pick for the best domain experts are QA engineers. These testers are used to working in the product from a user's perspective—all they do is test. It's counter-intuitive, but I find the QA engineers that are less technical—I mean the ones who don't write code all day—tend to be more knowledgeable in the product itself. Something about seeing the forest despite the trees, not getting lost in the weeds. We'll talk more about the value of manual testing, but for now, simply remember that domain expertise is important, and technical specialists like software engineers often don't have the same intuition of every business use case like a domain expert. The exception is senior employees who have been around forever and have seen it all.

2.3 Planning

Planning is where an engineer will be assigned to a set of work. The set of work should be carved out of the specification in a way that related work is grouped together in chunks that logically should be tackled all together and again divided up to be achievable in some reasonable timeline. The result will be a *development plan* for an individual chunk of work.

Engineers are the experts here, and they are the ones who know what needs to be done. They will likely sort out the work to either the resident expert on the team who is knowledgeable in that type or work or perhaps a more intrepid assignment to someone who wants to broaden their experience and work on a less familiar section of the system.

That's a lot of words to say the planning phase sets the promised deadline at the individual worker's level. A solid test plan is an important part of it.

At this point, the target version of the system is likely decided, and all the planning pertains to, let's say the next major version, or a minor version perhaps, but each chunk of work should have a target version set and ready.

Small changes here may add a seemingly trivial amount of work, for example, adding a testing requirement to the plan. Something like "Write a unit test." line item somewhere on the document, probably lonely and forgotten near the very bottom, an afterthought, with the implication being "if we get to it."

Now, suppose there are 50 engineers working on their development plans all at once, every two weeks, forever. That minor testing task represents quite a lot of total work hours at scale. Significant work hours like that shouldn't be left to capricious whims like "if we get to it." Leaders need to set policy. Test plans should be required, and time for them should be allocated.

Make testing a priority. It must be accounted for and considered for every single development plan. The good news here is that it's not always necessary! Perhaps the new work is already covered by some existing test, or maybe the work simply doesn't need to be tested. Changing some website copy text on a privacy policy page no one ever sees? You probably don't need to write an automated test for that. Business domain experts shine here as well.

At every development plan's inception, you want your engineers to ask themselves (and their peers) if they should be testing or not. This is a great opportunity to encourage ownership of the testing process by every single team member.

2.4 Development

Time to grind! Plans are developed. Specifications are ... specified.

The hacker puts on their headphones, and strange upbeat electronic dance music blasts through as code seemingly pours from their fingertips to the computer, pristine and syntactically colored. Of course, everything already works and there are no problems, at least not on my machine.

The hacker leans back, with complete confidence, and hovers over the "Push to GitHub, reintegrate and merge, skip code review and all tests" button.

But wait! Just for fun, let's test this seemingly perfect new code.

All those tests you write, every software engineer should run them on their machine before they send off their work. Every time. This is the point in the process where there are few exceptions to testing priority. Your engineer is about to send their work to merge together with everyone else's work. You really should test it as much as possible before that happens. This is the stage where mistakes are easiest to fix.

However, some types of tests take longer than others to run. Unit tests are very low-level code tests that run quickly, almost instantly. There are many other types of tests, and depending on the type of code your software engineer is focusing on at this particular chunk of the system, you should have a test plan in place to check their work before it goes out. You may have noticed the previous planning phase is where this testing plan should have been written. If you forgot to do it there, the engineer has to do it now, alone and under pressure to ship out their latest code. They will not get the benefit of time allocation if a plan has to be rushed last minute. Engineers sometimes realize this fact and will consequently sometimes start paying attention to testing in the planning phase. But sometimes, and all too often, they will simply blame management for unrealistic expectations. They do have a point.

When a software engineer (or anyone, maybe even you! Imagine.) tests the software on their machine, it's known as "testing locally." To make it happen, the "local" workstation needs some way to set up the application (or the relevant piece of the application) and run it under simulated conditions that are similar enough to real-world deployment that it can reasonably stand as a facsimile of the actual product. *Where* the application is running for testing is called an *environment*. Running locally is the "local environment." Running the actual product in the real world is generally called "production" or "the production environment."

There can be unlimited testing environments to be employed before production, whatever fits your need. We'll dig into the common options next.

Let's zoom back for a moment and realize what's happening at this stage in the software development lifecycle. New code exists. You want to move it to the next stage in the lifecycle, you want to get it out to production. Ship it! Before we do, it must be verified, it has to be tested.

We can hope (and pray) that our studious ~~Hackers~~ software engineers will test their work locally before it's merged with the other in-progress code. We can even insist they do so. We can send strongly worded emails. Begging and pleading? But wait, we can do better!

2.5 Staging: Internal

Staging, as in a stage before production. To stretch a theater metaphor, the dress rehearsal stage is set before we enact *the production* to a real audience.

"Staging" is a common term for an internal testing environment where all the new code your engineering team has produced is added to the product/application and continuously built and run in a *test environment.*

The advantage of this setup is you can use it to run tests on incoming code, and gleefully **deny** that code if it doesn't pass. Test failed, merge denied! Sometimes this is called "gating," as in a gate that can't be passed without proper credentials. Or an exclusive nightclub you can't enter unless the bouncer likes you. I personally wish code that fails to enter the party was referred to as "bounced" or "86'd," but I digress—terminology follows the trends of use.

ERROR: Test failed on line 134 on file/SomeBrokenFile.php

Imagine a software engineer seeing this error report. Their first thought is "Well what went wrong??" They would have just finished their work and thought it was good enough to ship. Most likely, they will examine the error and try to glean some information about which test failed and why.

Reading an error report from a failed test can be enlightening, but it can also be confusing or misleading. Sure, they might get a line number or code location. They may get 100 files and line numbers. The fact is, they need more context and addressable information. They really need to run the test *locally* and step through the process to determine where the failure occurred.

So our harried engineer will try to fix that file and send it right out again. This is a waste of time, they should run the test locally to see if it works before attempting another merge.

Require local tests! Encourage a culture of testing early and often. Even the longer-running tests should at least be available for individual engineers to run anytime. Arbitrarily. "Hey why not?" is the goal for ease of use. With modern tools, this process can be as simple as a single button press.

Even so, before merging into the staging environment, that same test gate should be run and deny new code that causes errors. This is where version control works together with test tools to handle code operations.

The application is now built and running, living in the staging environment. Most likely only accessible to the development team, quality assurance testers, and anyone else who wants a demonstration of the new work. Product owners, project managers, perhaps a support team representative who wants to check up on a bugfix. These are concerned parties *within* the organization.

At this point, your automated testing has made a best effort to test the system. All those "long-running" tests I mentioned, you can run them here and you should. Run everything! Give 'em hell. Put that new work through the ringer. Excellent, that's how the pros do it!

It's still not enough!

You might be able to take that staging environment and open it up to other parties, say a client or auditing authority. All well and good, but most organizations don't want to air their (potentially) dirty laundry and risk embarrassment in front of clients. Once we have a generally solid assurance of quality for our internal staging build, it might be time to expose that build to a select audience.

2.6 Staging: External

An external staging environment can be the ideal solution for showing off new work to clients, auditors, focus groups, etc. This should be a well-tested version of the product, and the environment itself should consider security for outside access. Be sure the only parties that can access your external staging environment are trusted and authenticated.

This phase of the software development lifecycle is interesting. Now you're collaborating with another team, another company, someone else.

How can we set mutual expectations for how the product should behave? The interested external party might want to test it themselves (imagine that!). You could offer to share all your hard-earned, painstakingly developed automated tests, but this is probably not practical. For one thing, test code closely describes your application code, which may be secret. Another problem is that your external tester may not use your particular software testing system at all, so the code and tests you have won't work for them easily.

The system itself behaves in a predictable way though. We know our product, so we can describe how it *should* work. We can do even better. Let's hand over the formal specification of behavior we worked on in the first phase of our lifecycle. That way, our external tester knows just what to expect. If everything went according to plan, that same specification is the one we designed with them in the first place.

Wouldn't that be nice?

2.7 Production

We've checked it internally, they tested it externally. A few bugs sent the code back, we fixed it or decided to ignore the problem. Let's ship it!

Now, the highest-stake testing begins. Real users. Actual customers. Here's where you will find everything you missed, every bug or complaint, legitimate or not. They're testing your code! Isn't that helpful? They might even report bugs they find on social media or the actual news if it's severe enough.

You will also find out what known bugs or questionable behavior is simply not an issue, ignorable. A major upside, pay attention to what is being tolerated.

Usage metrics, the measure of how your real users engage your bonafide production application is beyond the scope of our discussion here, but it can inform you of which parts of the system are important and which are less important. Which functions of your software make money and which do not. You should work to understand these questions and prioritize your testing effort accordingly.

We can wait for the real customers to test everything, and they will, don't worry. Plenty of organizations are also going to double check everything with a *user acceptance testing* team. UAT will look at the production application and engage like real users and test the system. This might be a separate testing team, or it could be the primary quality assurance team, depending on how your organization likes to use acronyms.

In fact, UAT as a team of testers might be deployed to test the system at any point in the lifecycle post-development. Indeed, an external testing UAT team might be employed by your client or auditor.

Let's examine the role of support in this phase of development. All those helpful customer complaints or concerns are going to be handled by someone, a dedicated support team if you're lucky. For a small company that might be you, or worst-case scenario the engineering team. Professional computer nerds don't typically enjoy engaging with the public.

Support is going to report new bugs found in the wild, after being politely informed of the issue by a calm and rational customer.

What happens next is relevant to testing. Often, the support representative will need to recreate the reported bug to confirm it's real. The easiest path to testing that bug is to leverage an automated test configured to recreate the specific scenario reported. For this work, your support team will need access to the automated test code and some internal testing environment. Maybe your support team can run an arbitrary test on the internal staging environment, great! But what version of the build is in that environment at that moment? When the previous set of work has been shipped to production, the new in-progress work will take its place in the staging environment. Now as always, you need to be aware of version control to properly track bugs across builds.

2.8 Retrospective

Retrospective as a phase of development is a ceremony in the agile project management methodology.

I don't consider it purely an agile concept though, it's the conversation you have after a big set of work is shipped out the door. Maybe that's an informal break room chat around the coffee machine:

> Employee: Wow that was a seamless release, nothing major broke! I guess that happens sometimes?

> Senior Employee: Yes well our boss is serious about testing and QA so this is our comfortable routine and I'm happy.

Or maybe the meeting is a more formal affair where the whole team sits down to introspect and discuss strengths and weaknesses, chances for improvement and appreciate what went right.

> Employee: That big feature was way more complex than we thought in planning, I had to ask for a lot of help just to get it done.

> Senior Employee: Yes, and I think it shows we need to refine our development plan process, we should do more investigation and planning before we get started on something so large.

> Project Manager: Agreed, I'm making a note for the next planning meeting. Y'all going to the end-of-sprint happy hour tonight?

Sometimes, perhaps things went badly, and we need to break down what happened and make a plan for improvement. That's not a fun meeting.

Either way, communications are happening. Ritual and routine can guide the conversation and keep it under control, focused and productive. Don't forget to celebrate! Remember the goal of all this process and testing. An uneventful, smooth product update is a very good thing.

2.9 Summary

- Test-driven development can be a difficult goal and not realistic for those new to testing.

- Focus on consistent testing across your software development lifecycle.

- Steps in the lifecycle correspond to different environments where your code runs.

- For each environment your software lives in, the version of your application must also be tracked.

- Tests you run against your application at any phase of the lifecycle will be run on a specific version of that application, in a specific environment.

- Clarify your development work with specifications, to describe system behavior and simultaneously outline a test plan.

- Pay attention to business domain experts—QA engineers are a good source.

- Every stage of the lifecycle has opportunities to prioritize testing.

- Planning is a good place to define specifications.

- Development is ideal for writing and running unit tests.

- Internal staging is where all tests can and should be run.

- External staging is a good place to share specifications with external testers.

- Production is where UAT may happen, and your end users will finally test your product.

CHAPTER 3

Quality and Assurance

This chapter covers disambiguation between terms and a high-level holistic perspective on software quality. Risk management through assurance, overview of techniques and methodologies.

3.1 What Does Quality Mean to You?

Quality is a subjective term, so you need to figure out what it means to you and your team. When you have a real definition of quality, only then can you provide assurance through testing.

Your team is going to look to you as a source of truth when it comes to quality standards. Without guidance, testing can be neglected, or it can get wild. Software engineers can demonstrate either extremes of quality concern for seemingly practical reasons.

On one hand, software is never truly done or perfect. There's always something to fix, something to refactor, some extra polish you can add, endless testing in every possible scenario, use case, or environment.

On the other hand, you need to ship something. Perfection is the enemy of progress. No one actually looks at the JavaScript errors your website throws to the console. Where even is the JavaScript console? We may never know.

© Ross Radford 2024
R. Radford, *Software Testing for Managers*, https://doi.org/10.1007/979-8-8688-0572-1_3

Consider your users, the people who interact with your software. They signed up or maybe even paid for your product! Do they care what shade of blue the "Buy Now!!" button is on every page? Maybe. Do they care if you sell their personal data to some sketchy data harvesting company? Probably. That might even be illegal—you should check into that. Let's get the government on the phone right now.

> Software Manager: Hey, The Government. Is it cool if I sell my user's personal data to someone else?

> The Government: Depends on the type of personal information. Health info, social security number, or something like that? Definitely not.

> Software Manager: Alright thank you...

> The Government: Wait. We have a contract with you for federal employee use of your system. According to our testing your website doesn't let me tab through the main menu using the keyboard.

> Software Manager: Um, is that bad?

> The Government: Yes, it doesn't meet accessibility standards! Also it's super easy to make that work. There's no excuse, you're so lazy! What is wrong with you??

> Software Manager: I DIDN'T TEST FOR ACCESSIBILITY. I'm so sorry.

> *gentle sobbing*

This embarrassing scene is avoidable.

3.2 Standards: You Should Have Some

You get to define what quality means to you and your team, but that will be informed by your clients, customers, competition, and general public sentiment. If your product works great but looks like it was designed in 1998, that's just not going to fly for most people. The government probably doesn't mind—they love a vintage software experience.

Externally facing, client or public accessible quality is the obvious focus for a business, maybe the top priority. Or so it may seem. You build an expectation of quality and strive to maintain it. This is why we test. Check to see the product is working as expected, performing up to expectations, and is reasonably aesthetically pleasing.

First, let's talk about internal standards you need to develop for your team. Expectations that must be met or there will be consequences. And what are those anyway?

The code your team generates should be held to some type of standard. To some degree, the system or language they code in will enforce rules, and messy, incorrect code simply won't work without throwing errors. You can set many language interpreters and compilers to a strict mode of code conventions, for even more opinionated structure, but this may be overkill if your current code is loosely defined. Keep in mind that if you decide to enforce strict rules, it may create a large set of work to bring your code up to that standard.

For engineers checking each other's work, there is a lot more to be done. "It works!" isn't enough. Code needs to be relatively readable, and that means different things to different teams. For some, it may mean breaking functions out into multiple methods if they get too long, such as multiple pages of code. For some, it may mean compliance with a strict specification set by the providers of your programming language itself.

We've all heard the hushed rumors and rare reports of some teams who actually document their systems. It's true, I've seen it myself!

This is largely ease of tool use and basic day-to-day work details for your engineering teams. They should be encouraged to set their own standards for what "good code" looks like. As a leader, you don't need to micro-manage these decisions, but you should keep an eye out for friction caused by rules that seem too rigid or hard for the team to follow.

The question for managers is this: How are the rules enforced? If a code review finds some work "functional, but not up to our code standards," what happens? Is the work rejected?

For a seasoned coder, well-formatted, standards-compliant, perfectly documented code might be the ideal panacea, but if it's taking too long to get there, consider marking it as an aspirational goal.

Security. More relevant every passing day, and I've seen quite a few passing days, let me tell you. Search for "data breach news" headlines and you'll get an idea of the state of the world.

Security in general is a huge complex topic, and the best advice I can give you is to contract expert firms to help. Third-party security auditors and advisors are more qualified than anyone you can hope to hire. Unless you're an actual security company, it's too much to handle yourself. Don't play games with the safety of your users or employees' data. Hiring a security expert full time is great, but don't expect to cover all the bases with one person. Know it's a bigger job than you can handle alone.

All that said, it's also extremely important to follow security best practices and do your best to educate yourself and your team. There are easy things you can do like keeping secret information such as passwords out of the code, checking your software dependencies for reported security issues, and using a password manager to generate strong passwords for all your important services. Now, take those post-it notes with your real login credentials off your office wall please.

You need to define what quality means to your team—they need a target to test against.

Undefined vague qualities like "It should just work!" are a fast way to waste time and money trying to test "everything." An unrestrained QA engineer will quickly show their creativity testing things you never even considered (every city field value on every form will be La Cañada Flintridge, California, or Hafnarfjarðarkaupstaður, Iceland). This is overkill—unless your customer base is Icelandic. Bring their zealous creative mind into a planning meeting to talk to the developers. Maybe that meeting could be an email, saving everyone time.

A classic example: Imagine a form element that collects a phone number. An unbound QA engineer might dream up endless scenarios to test the field, such as random letters and number combinations, phone numbers for a restaurant in Budapest, the timeless fake phone number 555-555-5555, and other scenarios. But is the code that validates the form *already being tested*? It's probably covered by unit tests on the code level, and if not, that's where you should focus your effort. Not on a parade of random data pushed through at the user interface level. In fact, it's very likely that such a form validation is performed by a common library that is already scrutinized by the providing organization. A software engineer will quickly sort out all these questions before your QA begins to run rampant.

This example highlights the need for collaboration between QA and developers, the need to specify test plans. You really should not be testing without a defined plan. All the more reason to focus on specifications. Define the expected behavior of your system and test against that.

3.3 Standards: Your Users

A service-level agreement is a promise your organization makes to another about consistency. If you're providing data or software as a service, you will both agree to terms on how often you provide service and how often your system may be unavailable.

These agreements are explicitly defined, so there's not much room for interpretation. How well your application can perform the service, or transfer of data, depends almost entirely on your infrastructure. It's usually an infrastructure issue that fails the agreement terms, but sometimes a bug or flaw in your software is causing an issue. That is obviously a high-priority bug!

There is a whole realm of testing for performance, which I won't get into. An advanced topic, mainly because untangling your testing target when it's code vs. infrastructure and environment, makes it a difficult pursuit. If you're sure you need this kind of testing, you need to rely on your most senior engineers to make a test plan and work with your operations team to set it up.

Unless your company is huge with tons of users, performance issues don't require testing at all—they're typically obvious as a quick logging inspection can point out timeout issues and problematic code that is throwing errors.

It's up to you to decide how long a user should wait for your application to do something.

It's also your decision which users or platforms are your target audience, and this has a huge effect on your testing effort. Do you need to support iPhones more than a decade old or web browsers that were around in 2010? If so, my condolences. Ask yourself, are you testing for platforms or users you really don't need to? It's a general rule that older or more obscure devices or platforms greatly increase testing effort. Most of the time, dropping support for these outliers can save you huge amounts of time and money.

The quality of service standards I'm describing here should be consistent across your organization. Who does your product serve, how fast is it, and what level of quality is expected? Try to get involved in the conversation—it will be happening from the highest level on down to the front lines.

Usability. How smooth and ergonomic is your product to actually use? If you have a slick graphic user interface, or even an API that provides data, the usability of that interface can be measured. There's plenty of theory out there, but the most important perspective comes from your users. How beautiful and intuitive do you want your product to be? Companies like Apple set a high bar, and that might be unrealistic unless usability is a big priority for your product.

Usability is a rabbit hole of deep learning, but whatever your goal there you need to define your standards of excellence for yourself.

3.4 Standards: The Government

3.4.1 HIPAA

If your company works with personal health data, you've no doubt heard of the Health Insurance Portability and Accountability Act (HIPAA). You've probably heard about it no matter what—it's definitely lodged in the public consciousness.

3.4.2 GDPR/CCPA

Maybe you know about the General Data Protection Regulation (GDPR) for European Union residents. Similarly, CCPA stands for California Consumer Privacy Act. A US state law to protect the data and privacy rights of California residents.

The end result is lots of annoying cookie compliance banners on websites these days, and hopefully, your company is doing it gracefully on your own website.

3.4.3 PCI DSS

If you're processing consumer payments as part of your regular business, you need to be Payment Card Industry Data Security Standard (PCI DSS) compliant. This one is a little tougher to pull off, but it can be done. If you screw it up, the PCI compliance motorcycle gang will send you emails, passive-aggressive insinuations, and demands of money.

3.4.4 Fair Credit Reporting Act

Working for a credit bureau, I got to learn all about the Fair Credit Reporting Act, which governs consumer credit data. Basically, if you are a credit bureau, there are rules. Simple enough.

I hope you enjoyed this short tour of fun and interesting data security standards, but we barely scratched the surface—there are many more. Whatever applies to your work, it's your job to learn about it and implement it, and how you do that is you educate your team. Let them know what they need to do and help translate the legal mandates into specifications, development plans, and test plans. These are requirements just as important as any others, and you can absolutely test them and assure compliance for every version of your software that ships.

3.4.5 Accessibility

Accessibility is a unique challenge, and I see it as an opportunity.

Accessibility I think is a typically confused topic in the software industry because it encompasses so many different concerns. Unless you're working for the federal government, you probably think of it as optional. Unless you're thoughtful about user experience, that is.

Have you thought about the experience of someone using your software through tools such as a screen reader? Would the elements be automatically translated to audio in the proper order?

How about someone colorblind? Would they be able to see all the important elements of your user interface easily?

Web Content Accessibility Guidelines (WCAG) are a great place to start to get familiar with these issues. A set of guidelines to help you understand accessibility with a focus on websites. The principles apply to most types of software and are worth digging into.

I humbly offer the perspective that accessible design is just plain good product design. A user who needs proper keyboard navigation for an app is not necessarily an atypical user. I want it. I want to tab through a menu or list of form options, personally, and I'm not alone. If your forms are unusable without a mouse to click through a basic list, I will tell you right now I absolutely will notice and think less of your work. Proper accessibility makes the experience better for everyone. Easy, intuitive user experience is everyone's goal, and more to the point, it's almost trivial to make it happen.

Are you unsure if your system is meeting accessibility guidelines? Test it!

3.5 Assuring Yourself

Setting in place your organization's standards for quality, now you have what you need to provide assurance. Confidence in your product's quality and your team's ability to reliably deliver that product, what could be sweeter?

To assure yourself, you're going to need metrics and reports. As a software leader, you'll be showing these to your boss and other less technical people in the company, and let's be clear, you need to see the data at a high level, most of the detail summarized for consumption.

Here, test coverage and code coverage become shorthand heuristics to help you make decisions. Chapter 5 is all about coverage, but for now, just know it's a summary of your testing efforts. This is much more complex than pass or fail. Recall the previous explanation of testing across different versions and environments. There is a potential for overlap in testing effort, which is essentially redundant work. Also, there is potential for low-priority testing to eat up time in your software development lifecycle.

Coverage is absolutely necessary to track for each and every version of your product, but it can only hint toward the quality of your tests themselves.

If you're testing for external standards like PCI or WCAG, more than likely you're also going to be audited by some external authority. In that case, you should test for compliance whenever possible in your development cycle, but that might be less frequent, depending on how demanding those tests are. For example, if you're audited for accessibility compliance annually, you might not bother testing for it every two weeks.

I don't think I need to explain that waiting until the last minute to test is a bad strategy. The usual truism goes like this: The last 20% of development ends up taking 80% of the time. Implicit blame is placed on testing in that saying, and the assumed system flaws it exposes. A salient point.

3.6 Business Domain Experts

I mentioned domain experts in Chapter 2, individuals who know your system inside and out and can casually chat about almost any user experience workflow from memory, with the caveats and sidebar context that even the product owner teams might not have.

Sometimes the best domain experts aren't obvious, but they are usually the most senior individuals at your organization. My pick is senior QA or UAT engineers—they see the product from many angles but don't necessarily know how the internal guts fit together. This provides a rare focus on usability and business use cases.

Solution architects, product owners, and yes even support staff are great sources of domain expertise. You need these experts to write accurate specifications, but there's another value to identifying them.

Automated testing isn't always available. Maybe the tests you need simply don't exist yet. Your test suite, or part of it, could be broken. Okay, it's nearly guaranteed that at least some part of your testing code will be unusable at any given point in time. Perhaps some test is marked to be ignored until the underlying system is repaired, and until then, it's going to throw a guaranteed error/failed test result you don't need. If you are certain a test will fail, there's not much point in running it.

There are many reasons you might be missing automated test coverage for some part of the system, but often at the same time, you need to test it anyway!

Here's where you call over your domain experts, and they help you design a specification or manual test plan. We will talk specifically about how to leverage manual tests in the next chapter. Just remember that broken automated tests don't mean you have to abandon your coverage and assurance.

3.7 New Bugs and Regressions

The goal of testing is quality assurance, to assure you that the system is working as expected.

However, the direct result of testing is *either* assurance *or* identifying bugs. When a test fails, don't shoot the messenger—that test is providing the value it was meant for.

When you find a new bug, it's either a brand new species or the much more common "Hmm this used to work fine, what happened?" otherwise known as *regression*.

Regressions are frustrating. Fixing the same bug more than once, even more so. Seeing the same bug for the fifth time, well that's a real exercise in higher-order emotional regulation.

If you see a previously fixed bug pop up again, either you didn't fix it right the first time, or a recent change that perhaps seemed unrelated is causing problems. Sometimes, if you're very unlucky, a previous bug fix gets undone by improper version control use. It happens.

Where regressions are annoying at best, new bugs are at least a little more interesting.

Both scenarios play out in the same way. A test, or worst-case scenario a user in production, finds a bug. Someone, probably a support representative, will confirm the bug is real and then send it to your engineering team for a fix.

As an aside, confirming that a bug is legitimate is an important first step. Whomever first encountered the bug should try to recreate it if possible. Sometimes, the bug is actually the result of bad information, like a misconfigured application or a typo in some user data input. The first question you should always ask the person who logged the bug is "what happened when you reproduced the issue?"

Occasionally, you'll get a bug report that is actually a request for a feature.

> User: Hey your system is broken! It doesn't allow me to upload photos of my cat to the internet like facebook does. Fix it.

> Support Rep: Sir this is Domino's customer support and the online pizza ordering was never meant to do that. Would you like to make a feature request to our development team?

User: Yes, do that. I'll wait.

Support Rep: I'll connect you with our Director of Software Engineering immediately, please hold. I think it's their day off, I'll try their cell phone.

If the bug is real, however, it will be passed on to the development team, hopefully in some kind of ticket tracking system, also hopefully with all pertinent information and related data to recreate the bug on a local system for confirmation. Reproduction steps and error logs go a long way to eliminate time-wasting back and forth when fixing a bug.

"Issue closed, cannot reproduce." is a common result of a bug that can't be demonstrated in the system. Fair enough. I also hope they write that on my tombstone as a testament to my unique character and contributions to society.

But let's say it's a real bug, and we can recreate it. Next, we have to *triage* the issue and understand it so we can try to fix it. A borrowed medical term exposes the sense of urgency this process usually takes place under.

Once we have an idea of the underlying cause, we can either fix it immediately or, if we're feeling more professional and strategic, prioritize and schedule it for development work.

When the bug is being fixed, just like all other development work, it should be considered for ongoing testing. Decide if it should be, and if so, write a test for it, and add that test to be run during the development phase. This is how you kill a regression with finality.

3.8 Location, Location, Location

Different test types locate bugs in the code more or less accurately. The main factor is proximity to code. Imagine it like this: how close to the code each test can get. Every level of abstraction away from the code reduces the precision of a test's ability to find that problematic line or routine or missing file.

By no means does that fact assume more precision is ideal. Without abstraction, you have too much granularity and you can't see the forest for the trees or simulate the user's experience. If you're too busy checking each leaf and bark pattern for beetles, you may not notice the smoke billowing over the next ridge. "Smoke test" is a common metaphor for stepping back and looking to see if the whole damn mess isn't obviously on fire when you turn it on. It can be a useful starting place.

All levels of visibility are vital, each has the tradeoff of precision over *coverage* area—Chapter 6 *covers coverage* by the way.

Unit tests are closest to the code, the least abstract form of testing. A unit test will ideally target a single code block and assert only a few lines of code, drastically reducing the search space when that test breaks.

Integration tests are the next level up, assuring two or more subsystems are working in harmony. This is where it gets a bit more abstract, because two interoperable pieces of code might both be perfectly correct, but some misalignment of configuration or other logical error breaks a test. That logical error won't be caught by unit tests, but will be found by integration tests. In triage, the investigating engineer will need to understand both interacting systems, and so this type of bug is harder to pin down.

Functional or UI testing is the next level of abstraction, testing from the user interface directly. These tests rely on our detailed understanding of expected behavior. Also important are error messages or codes, sometimes hidden from an actual user but available to the test if we know where to look. Broken tests here can be some of the most challenging to decipher. For example, one extremely common error state in a web application is a blank page, stark nothing staring you in the face. We know the login form *should* be there, but what the heck?

As we climb the abstraction steps, the harder it gets to find exactly what happened behind the scenes. Test types have different tradeoffs, and they support each other, filling in gaps.

3.9 User Acceptance Testing

UAT is testing from the perspective of the user, what a real user would see interacting with the system. You may have a whole separate UAT team separate from the other QA engineers—some companies make this separation of concerns as a sort of double-check on the work of the QA team, since they are by necessity closely enmeshed with the software engineers. And as I mentioned earlier, clients or other external concerns may have their own UAT team to evaluate your product. In that case, it would be prudent to anticipate and even recreate their testing methodology yourself before you send it out.

A UAT team, or a QA team putting on another hat and doing UAT testing, will have their own set of tests. Manual tests where they work through the product as a typical user would. These tests should be based on specifications of system behavior.

Another reason specifications are valuable is versatility for tasks just like this—you can share the work between teams and everyone benefits.

Keep in mind UAT is one of the most labor-intensive types of testing. As such, you want to carefully prioritize UAT testing time and look for chances to automate at least some parts of it.

If you do have a dedicated UAT team, consider that they are even further removed from the deep dark woods of code than your QA team. These are consummate business domain experts, and you can leverage that expertise.

3.10 Dashboards and Reports

What could be more lovely than a big appetizing pie chart showing all your automated test results?

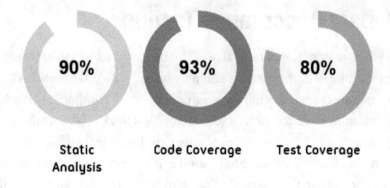

Static Analysis **Code Coverage** **Test Coverage**

Organized by environment, version numbers clearly labeled. Bright hues of green passing tests, red failed tests, yellow skipped, and gray ignored tests. A breathtaking tableau. Updating in real time, giving you a moment by moment bird's-eye view of the entire system. Glorious.

This data can allow you to make complex decisions like "Should we ship the product?" or not.

It's all so beautiful, there can't be any downsides. Please don't break my heart, I need those green pie charts like I need air. Are there any downsides?

Yes, there are. I'm so sorry.

First of all, that data needs to be collected, compiled, and transported for your dashboard software. Straightforward enough, but consider that it takes engineering work, which of course means ongoing maintenance.

Perhaps less obvious is the risk of over-assurance, a false sense of security.

Remember that your dashboard is going to show you test coverage in the terms you define. Is a passing test providing "coverage" in your view?

I'll reiterate that test coverage says nothing of test quality. This becomes important when you're trying to achieve assurance. You may have plenty of tests but are your tests actually good? Are they doing their job? Are they run consistently?

One possible pitfall here is when your team knows you're looking at the high-level view, they can easily rush through low-quality tests that pass and look good on the chart. In Chapter 5, we will explore coverage and all it means, but for now, I'll leave you with this scrap of cynical wisdom:

Goodhart's Law: When a measure becomes a target, it ceases to be a good measure.

3.11 Summary

- Quality is a subjective term—you need to figure out what it means to you and your team.

- Your code should be held to some type of standard you define.

- It's extremely important to follow security best practices and do your best to educate yourself and your team.

- You should not be testing without a defined plan.

- There are many security standards you need to know depending on the type of data your software works with.

- Test coverage and code coverage are heuristics to help you make decisions about quality assurance.

- The direct result of testing is either assurance or identifying bugs.

- Different test types locate bugs in the code more or less accurately.

- Unit tests are the most precise locators of bugs and cover the smallest area of the system.

- Integration and functional tests are more abstract and therefore less precise to locate problem code but cover more of the system at once.

- User acceptance testing is testing from the perspective of the user.

- Dashboards and reports are great but have a cost and can become a misdirection.

CHAPTER 4

Specification

This chapter explains how to specify system behavior to make the system testable. Unspecified system behaviors are not testable.

4.1 Roadmaps, Stories, and Behavior

Who starts new work on your product? Ultimately it's the customer, the one who pays. Someone is going to talk to the customer, hopefully a solution architect or product representative, or, worst case, sales.

Just kidding sales people. I know you're important, but you tend to promise the moon.

Whoever brings the new work has an idea of what the new system behavior will be. The "system" being your software.

Maybe your client wants a new button on your app. That's a nice ambiguous goal, let's run with it!

> Product Owner: Okay we need a new button on this screen, it should be greenish-blue and deactivate registration when clicked.

> Lead Engineer: Alright, we've done buttons before, we can handle it.

> Product Owner: Great, I'll review when development is complete. See you in two weeks!

© Ross Radford 2024
R. Radford, *Software Testing for Managers*, https://doi.org/10.1007/979-8-8688-0572-1_4

The problem with this transaction is the lack of detail, the *undefined behavior* of the new feature.

Later, when the engineer in the above scenario is "done," that's when all the important questions will finally get asked.

What does this new button do? What happens when it gets a click? What if the user is automatically disqualified from using it? Error messages? You get the idea, there are many cases to consider, and it can be tempting to make assumptions to move things along.

If you've been building software for a while, you know what happens if you don't set clear expectations. Nothing is decided, and that means the *scope* of work can change constantly. Scope tends to creep outward, it grows when you're not watching it carefully.

In the real world, no matter what, there's almost always some degree of change in expectations along the way as things get built. It's a fact of life and we should accept it, but also aggressively minimize scope as much as possible while delivering high-quality work, and the best way to do that is to set clear expectations.

Our best bet is to agree on the work. Both from the product request side and the development side, and every step of the way along the multiple handoffs as software is built, tested and delivered.

Recall how in Chapter 2 we illustrated how the steps of the software development lifecycle are each driven by people. In our contrived example above, there's only two people discussing the new product behavior. That's a problem, because every single person involved should have a detailed plan of what the new behavior is.

Consider how the individual software engineer needs clearly defined system behavior requirements most of all, to be sure they are building the right thing. Everyone who will check the work needs it as well.

When the new system behavior is hammered out, it should also be taken back to the customer/client for agreement. When the code development work is complete, it needs to be tested, and the **ONLY** way to test it adequately is to compare the new behavior against the requirements. There should be a detailed description of new system behavior that an engineer can check against. Even the product owner in our example will later need to sign off on the new work, and these are busy people with many irons in the fire. A couple weeks of development time is more than enough to make anyone second-guess their own memory of a conversation.

Crystalize that behavior definition and make sure everyone concerned has access to the plan. Agile or other planning process is a key part of defining behavior here, and it should be well defined even before the new work request is handed to the engineers for development.

We can specify new behavior by creating a *specification*. Specs can be quite formal; there are countless templates for software specification, but unless you already have a mandate to use a particular type, I strongly recommend *Specification by Example*.

4.2 *Specification by Example*: Book Reference and Summary

Usually, when a software engineer suggests I read a book, it's an unsubtle way of saying I should "go educate myself."

I will actually read any book. Especially when it's a semi-polite suggestion that I'm missing some key ideas.

One book changed my outlook on software so dramatically, I can't talk about high-level testing strategy without mentioning it: *Specification by Example* by Gojko Adzic, published June 6, 2011, ISBN 978-1617290084.

Testing software effectively requires that you know in detail how the application is meant to behave.

The techniques presented in the book are almost exclusively based on real-world examples, with full accounts in the quoted words of the actual companies who found success by defining specifications for their software.

After working with these ideas directly for many years, I'm convinced. This is how software development should be done. Specifications should be recorded in concise plain language, with key examples for each software feature.

A simplified example:

> **Given** a website user
>
> **When** I successfully login to the website
>
> **Then** I should see a welcome message popup
>
> **And** the message should contain my name

Given When Then language is an idiomatic grammar where system behavior is defined and automated code can be directly linked and executed. But the scenario stands alone with or without automation. We'll dig more into *Given When Then* specifications later in this chapter.

This specification forms an incredible living documentation that empowers:

Product Owners: Who have a unified language to describe application features with every other part of the organization, including clients.

Developers: Who can clearly understand and reference the new work asked by clients and further can directly automate the specification as a test.

Project Managers: They can get a clear, granular view of which requirements are in progress, complete, or tested.

Quality Engineers, Software Engineers in Test, User Acceptance Engineers: A clear, settled example of application behavior makes testing faster and less confusing.

Note   If you are already writing user stories like this, great, but user stories alone are not enough to get the full benefits of specification. There must be a unified effort across your organization. Starting from initial feature design, through development to quality assurance testing where the specification is the document of truth.

What does this have to do with testing?

Tests without defined behavior are vague—their value is hard or impossible to quantify.

Specifications are also a kind of test plan—they describe test steps and can be used for manual testing.

Automated tests that break (and they certainly will break) can fall back on these specifications for much faster manual testing while the automation is being fixed. This is an important benefit of defined behavior, don't overlook it. I guarantee it will happen regularly.

4.3 Unknown Unknowns: Unspecified System Behaviors Are Not Testable

I enjoy using a simple login form in examples. Everyone is familiar with them and can picture one easily. Useful in discussions as an example entry to a larger system.

Login screens represent a basic user input interface and a lot of background plumbing for security. When you login to a system, a session is created, and that will be part of all your interactions until you log out. These are all separate functions of the system overall, but the login form is where the magic starts, and it's just as crucial a part of the system as any, a confluence of security, user experience design, input handling, and of course everyone's favorite: gracefully presented helpful error messages in precisely the right shade of red.

In the future, always seemingly just a few short years away, we may not use usernames and passwords. We'll use federated user credentials and some kind of passkey token or some other better system yet to be invented. That's the fun of predicting the future, uncertainty! If the classic dyad of username/password input goes away, the login page will persist; even if it becomes merely a login button on some other welcome page that scans your retinal signature. A bright future indeed. For now, bear with me and picture a standard login page as we sail into the unknown.

Let's talk about "fuzzing." Fuzzing is a method of testing user inputs by trying extreme boundaries. For example, a username input field where we try to input the maximum number of characters with an absurdly long, obviously fake username.

Username: "AAAAAAAAAAAAAAaaaaaaaaaaaaaaaaaaaaaaaaaaaaaaaa aaaa293876497uywdk"

You get it. This is such a common idea that I've found many people think of this fuzzing concept as quality assurance in a nutshell. For some reason, our minds tend to land here when we think about testing, but if you undergo any serious software testing effort, you quickly discover that tests like this are a waste of time. Let me explain.

There are two main reasons we don't need tests like this. First and most practically, the functionality is probably already being tested! If you don't know, well that's your new task, to find out.

Imagine a login form on a web page. You can easily limit the number of characters in the input with simple HTML; let's say we limit the username to 30 characters. Do we need to build a test that enters 31 characters just to be sure the web browser is actually working to limit that field? No, the browser is doing the work and has been tested extensively by a very large and concerned company. Now, after the login screen, beyond the form input, the data the user typed in will be sent to another part of the system, and it needs to be sanitized and checked at that point too. Here's where things get more complicated, and this is where an engineering team comes in to help. A testing-aware engineer knows testing effort should be evaluated for higher-priority goals, and frivolous tests should be prevented. Defer to the experts, and communicate the shared intent to make testing itself more worthwhile and higher quality on your team.

Consider: Are we building our login form absolutely from scratch code without relying on third-party (probably open source) libraries or frameworks? There are exceptions, but I'm going to jump to a conclusion and say *no*. Most likely, we're using an existing login template with input validation built in. That code is covered by tests the vendor authors use for their own quality assurance before shipping it out to the world. You don't need to test *their* system through *your* system for every possible use case. Come up with a few focused test cases that are directly relevant to your business use cases, and that's probably enough. Ask your engineers: is the input validation done by some library? It absolutely should be, unless your organization itself is a security tool software vendor. Now, we need to learn more about package management and where we actually get our code from and how to best know it's secure and tested. Security testing is a deep topic, and Chapter 7 is dedicated to just that.

Building everything yourself from scratch is rarely justified, but sometimes it will be, and if you're in this predicament, feel free to go nuts with the fuzzing. Fuzz away! But this probably isn't true, and you can easily check to see if your input validation is already covered by tests.

The other reason we don't need fuzzing is a little more philosophical but stay with me here because we're encompassing a larger point.

Bugs, by definition, are unexpected system behavior. To some degree, we see bugs coming a mile away anyway, especially when we're falling behind on quality assurance and testing. That enrollment workflow we didn't fully test but pushed out anyway? Brace for impact.

Error states are catch-all categories for unplanned system behavior we can anticipate, the known unknowns.

Then, there's all the bugs we *can't* anticipate. Unknown unknowns. Now and in the future, we simply can't test for every possible bug. The bugs we can anticipate are a much smaller set of possibilities and are therefore an attainable target. Existing system behavior should inform your testing before all else.

Fuzzing is unfocused. It's a kind of "well let's try this and see what happens" guesswork which isn't a real plan.

We can test all the *parameters* of an input with a *parameterized* test that draws on a large set of organized input to try, that's a better approach. Even so, consider the output of a large set of parameters for a single test, say 1000. What if 30 of those fail? You'll have to find the common pattern and determine if it's a true bug or not. Now, consider this parameterized testing across your entire application. The results stack up quick, and now you have an engineer sifting through giant tables of results searching for some unknown pattern. What's the return on investment from all that time and effort?

An even better idea is to consider the value of testing the input at all. What's really happening when someone enters an invalid username? What should happen is a valid user logs in, and any other invalid input throws an error. Do we care if the invalid input is ten characters or five hundred? No. It makes more sense to start with a test for the valid user and one to represent all invalid cases, to make sure the error is presented. Simple and effective, with results we anticipate.

QA engineers will happily explore the depths of human imagination trying to break your software any way possible and will never tire or run out of invented scenarios that can passably resemble a coherent testing plan. As a manager, know that this misguided work can become a huge distraction with an unlimited scope. It's important to prioritize your testing effort, and the best way to do that is to focus on coverage of the known system behavior. Once you have satisfactory coverage, we can absolutely go above and beyond, but that will be a waste of time if we miss the basics. Testing effort needs close project management to stay on track, just like all software development.

Fuzzing doesn't have a clear goal in mind, it's undirected testing of single cases that may or may not be relevant to our testing goals and priorities. We can stab in the dark testing extremely niche edge-cases like the user trying to set their username to all eggplant emojis, or we can test what we know.

To do that, we need to define system behavior. This is another value of writing specifications. Project management can bring order to the chaos and give us a clear expectation of how things should work.

Security testing is an exception in many ways. Security testing can justify getting more exploratory and aggressive, and we'll talk about it in Chapter 7.

4.4 Refactoring

Refactoring means changing how your code works, but with the same inputs and outputs remaining. Think of it as an in-place replacement.

The risk of course is new code. I'm building emotional stress just thinking about it.

Refactoring is sometimes painful, but it is frequently necessary. Upgrading software component versions is a good example. Another might be an optimization effort to make code more efficient or secure or simply easier to read. Believe me, it can get messy.

We mentioned earlier the standards you may place on your code, perhaps a stricter level of the language specification, which will require tighter code style and conventions. Style itself may be enforced through automation. Whitespace rules, comment structure, dependency injection requirements, there are a lot of possibilities. These rules don't necessarily affect the logic of the underlying code, and so should be considered a secondary priority. To that end, when your team commits code to "make it pretty," those changes should be committed separately from changes to the underlying logic if possible. Things like indentation fixes and renaming variables for clarity are less urgent but still important changes. The risk of introducing bugs can be greatly reduced with testing in place.

Everything about refactoring gets easier with testing. Writing new code that should act the same way as old code is just about the most straightforward application of a test there can be.

Zoomed out, looking at the system from a higher level, we can define system behavior with specifications that will allow larger more extensive changes and still give us a reasonable amount of assurance for maintained functionality.

This way, you can update old systems more easily and safely.

4.5 Upgrades

Overheard in the office on a calm and sunny Friday afternoon in spring:

> Software Engineer: Did you hear about the new security vulnerability found in that node package?

> QA Engineer: Which package was it?

> Software Engineer: Looks like... about 10,000 of them. We're using two. Apparently they have it fixed in the new versions already.

> QA Engineer: Are you going to upgrade today then? Please wait until next week.

> Software Engineer: Don't worry, we have that part of the system covered.

> QA Engineer: Show me.

And so it was.

Changing the version number on your application's components can be nerve-wracking. Is this going to break everything?

Some minor upgrades fix trivial bugs and are a safe bet, so much so you can accept them as part of your build process without a lot of hassle. You can specify in your dependency management system project configuration file (also called the *manifest*) exactly which minor upgrades to accept automatically. You'll need to decide if that convenience is worth the minor risk of possible new bugs. More substantial upgrades require more consideration.

Let's imagine there's a recommended security upgrade to your form input validation library. In this hypothetical case, it's a recommendation but not urgent, maybe an edge case vulnerability. You make the prudent decision to try the upgrade.

At least you know the affected part of the system: form input. You can run unit tests on the input processing on the back end, integration tests on any API responses that may send you input, and some functional test scenarios anywhere the form validation is used on the user interface. That's not so bad—we know where to test after the upgrade.

Now, let's suppose you need to upgrade your language version, which could potentially affect just about every single line of code in your application. Yikes. Wait, let's not panic, we can read the release notes included along with every upgrade that will detail all major changes and bug fixes.

When you need to upgrade a dependency, you can estimate the risk involved by reading the release notes and consider the area of your system that could be affected. For a minor upgrade or a sparsely used dependency, this is pretty straightforward and you can probably treat it like other refactoring work. Make the change, test it, and commit. For a major upgrade, a safer process is recommended.

Assign a senior engineer to do some research and read the release notes, maybe search online for common known upgrade problems and build an upgrade plan. There's likely to be some obvious changes you need to make on your system right out of the gate. Now that you have an idea of the changes involved, you can start a major upgrade testing effort. For each of the obvious upgrade tasks, see if you can get those into the existing system while still maintaining functionality and make those changes, testing as you go. With the known work done, and a development plan defined, we can get started with the actual upgrade. But first!

I hope by now you can see where this is going and anticipate the requirement: coverage. For each upgraded part of your system, you need tests that cover it as much as possible. You must have a fairly comprehensive testing suite to test a large change like the base language version or a framework upgrade. Write your tests.

Now with tests armed and ready, allocate a special staging environment for the upgrade. Create a separate branch of your code to work with and upgrade your versions in your dependency management configuration (manifest) file for that branch. The challenge here is your comprehensive testing will probably output a fair amount of bugs which may or may not be related to your upgrade. You'll be seeing all the current bugs in that branch as well. That will take time and effort to sort out. You'll need to also keep your upgrade code branch in sync with your main development branch. Rely on your version control experts for these maneuvers. While you sort out a potentially large set of reported errors, time will pass, and the main development branch will be adding and fixing code, so you'll need to keep in sync as much as possible. When you've made the upgrade, tested, and fixed all the bugs (or all the ones you care about), it's time to merge in the upgrade! Don't merge this beast on a Friday afternoon, take my word for it.

Major upgrades are a jarring and somewhat tense process made vastly more comfortable with comprehensive testing. Minor dependency upgrades can be smooth and sometimes a complete non-issue when you're lucky, but isn't it nice to know if they do cause an issue you'll detect it early with testing?

4.6 Given, When, Then

User stories are a popular pattern in project management these days, and you might have encountered them in a *Given, When, Then* format.

Given a new customer is seated at the restaurant

When the customer places an order

Then send the order to the chef

This could be a real scenario for a restaurant point of sale system. Theoretically, this could even be used to formally manage a restaurant ordering flow without software at all. I'm not a chef, so let's stick with software for now.

Per our previous discussion about specification, it should be obvious how user stories written with Given, When, Then can also be a behavior specification. They can be! But there are some differences and more importantly things to avoid.

User stories don't have to perfectly describe use cases, they can be quite vague, with the idea that more detail will be attached to the story in project management software. In this way, user stories can simply be a type of high-level summary, which I will admit is quite useful to communicate the overall intent of the work. Still, this nebulous style of behavior definition has limited ability to provide a testing plan.

User stories that also serve as *specifications* are far more valuable, and they have a special super power: they can act as test scenarios. In fact, there are software testing systems that can directly translate your Given, When, Then Language into code! Don't get too excited though, it's not magic. For every Given statement, you'll need to add code that connects the dots in your particular system. There is immense value to this method, and I'll get more into why in Chapter 5.

Let's break our restaurant example down to show what it represents in the context of software testing. Each statement describes behavior and is very useful as is, but I'll also explore the implications of building out an automated test for each.

Given a new customer is seated at the restaurant

In restaurant point of sale software, this could mean a server clicked a button on a table layout diagram indicating a new customer is getting ready to order, reserving that table and opening a new tab.

If we were setting up an automated test, this would entail creating a new fake customer session, assigning that user a seat on our table layout system, and generally getting the system into the expected state, ready to place an order.

When the customer places an order

Well we know which customer, because it's the one we set up with the Given statement. Open a tab. Now, we just need to add some things to it. Here, "an order" isn't exactly specific, that could be anything, but for the purpose of the specification, the order should be passed on to the chef no matter what it is. As long as the order is valid enough to be passed on, it's sufficient to test that functionality. To be clear, we're not testing that the items we add to the order are on the menu, and we're not testing that we can open a tab, we're assuming all that stuff already works.

For an automated test, we access the new tab data holder we opened and add some token menu item to it. Let's say a taco and a margarita, and some chips for the table. First, we would be sure those items are actually on the menu, or else this whole scenario would error out real quick, and we're not testing the menu system here. We could check for the item in the menu system by looking it up in the menu item list and asserting it exists there. But this is not recommended because if the item changes in the future, the test will then break without reaching the target state.

Then send the order to the chef

Let's say there's some kind of chef notification service, and we now pass the order to it. This is a single order, so we're not closing the tab. For this scenario, we've defined the proper behavior and we're done.

For an automated test, we pass the order to the chef notification service, and now, we have the system in the proper state to finally test our use case. For each test, there should be one target state. Now, we can verify the order is passed to the chef notification service. This is done with an assertion statement, that will either pass or fail, and this final target state is the only place where we should assert anything. Notice this final **Then** statement represents the target system state where the test takes place—the rest was all preparation. After the test, there might be a little data management like resetting the fake customer, possibly erasing them from the system and deleting the new, unfinished tab we created.

Let's look at another example where we have way too much happening.

Given a new customer is seated at the restaurant

When the customer places an order

And the order asks for chips

And the order asks for two house margaritas

And one of the margaritas should not have salt

And the order asks for a dozen tacos

And the order asks for something not on the menu like a balloon animal

And they want separate checks

And they want flan for dessert

And they want espresso but will settle for coffee

Then send the order to the chef

All these **And**s build a huge order that is really more than we need to test that the order was sent to the chef. If it's not obvious, the reason is because those **And** statements are implying assertions at every step of our setup. That's way too many assertions and it's too much extraneous information.

The scenario is confusing in purpose and execution and fails to describe the specification of sending an order to the chef, the order itself isn't needed to describe that behavior.

Imagine this specification is hooked up to automation. Every one of those menu items is accessed in code and added to the order. It's not clear what is required and what is optional. As an automated test, the **And** statements are implied as necessary, and so this test has many hurdles to jump before it can make the final assertion, greatly increasing the chance something will fail, or maybe just taking longer than necessary. Worst case, each of those orders is intended as an assertion: A hard stop if it fails. Essentially this verbose specification is trying to test the ordering system and several menu components at once. That's a problem for several reasons. The main one is that the test is too busy and unfocused. If something breaks in the espresso ordering system and an assertion catches that unrelated bug, the test will fail early and will never complete the primary objective.

Unnecessary complexity alone is a good reason to target only one assertion per test, but there are many more as we will see, including test reuse!

4.7 Summary

- Unspecified system behaviors are not testable.

- There should be a detailed description of new system behavior that an engineer can check against.

- I strongly recommend *Specification by Example* as a methodology.

- Book: *Specification by Example* by Gojko Adzic, published June 6, 2011, ISBN 978-1617290084.

- Given When Then language is an idiomatic grammar where system behavior is defined, and automated code can be directly linked and executed.

- Every individual involved with software development benefits from specifications.

- Specifications are also a kind of test plan, they describe test steps, and can be used for manual testing.

- Fuzzing is a method of testing user inputs by trying extreme boundaries. Not recommended.

- Refactoring means changing how your code works, but with the same inputs and outputs remaining.

- Everything about refactoring gets easier with testing.

- Testing also takes the worry out of dependency upgrades.

- Excessively long Given, When, Then specifications are not recommended.

- Each test should have one target state, and usually one assertion with some exceptions.

CHAPTER 5

Automation Reuse

This chapter explains how to leverage test code across the entire organization and beyond.

I want to share a story about the transformative power of testing I witnessed first-hand.

My company had a list of formatted test data we emailed around on an Excel spreadsheet. This data was used to test certain parts of the system. When something broke or needed to be verified, we fired up the spreadsheet, found the data we needed, and plugged it into the website to recreate certain scenarios.

As you might imagine, keeping this info current was a constant headache. Who has the latest version? A game of telephone might clue you in, or maybe not. Not to mention, when one set of data was in use by someone, no one else could use that data. Making changes to the data required a phone call and up to 48 hours, after which a new spreadsheet would be mailed out and passed along. I'm not joking, that was real.

I was working on a program that needed some of that data, an automated testing suite. I'd copy some of the data out of the spreadsheet, send out a mass email begging everyone who used it "*Please do not* touch user data rows 300–350!!" and then I'd pray my system didn't break due to someone messing with my user data.

Funny enough, it was this very anxiety that inspired a system to manage that data, tracking which data set was in use and even eventually working with other back-end systems to create or delete data as needed. It was beautiful.

R. Radford, *Software Testing for Managers*, https://doi.org/10.1007/979-8-8688-0572-1_5

But that wasn't the big revelation, and really I didn't expect anyone to use an automated system that fed data to my tests. It's a little esoteric for even the geekiest engineers.

What changed everything was a simple internal website where everyone emailing around that test data could simply click a button to get what they needed. One click. The data they received was up to date and managed to prevent overlap. It was a major hit. The entire support team, account managers, and about 50 people total all switched overnight. Their jobs got easier and *much* faster. No more phone calls, no more emailing, no more local copies of outdated spreadsheets, no more waiting days to get data changes.

Here's the funny thing: no one mentioned it. My team didn't even know who was using it, until we decided to analyze the network traffic and sort by department. I remember seeing those numbers for the first time. Suddenly comprehending the value of what we had built. I went around asking people what they liked, getting feedback, grinning and laughing.

Automated testing and indeed the test data itself can have outsized value to any organization, if you know how to use and reuse it.

5.1 Be Less Assertive

Tests break. When your test breaks, by fail or error, further assertions in that test are never executed.

Any single assertion depends on one single *state* of the system under test. So, I recommend limiting your tests to one single *target state* per test as a central philosophy. Getting your system into one target state is an extremely useful side effect of testing, one that you can isolate and reuse.

Related, but not the same thing are assertions, which you should also limit to one per test if possible. However! There are cases where you might need multiple assertions, such as a complex target state with many aspects that should get tested like a target data object being tested for multiple elements.

The issue is that assertions will do their job, which is to break and find bugs. When a test failure happens, traditional assertions will halt test code execution. The target state of the system is the final crucial context of the test, and it would be ideal to have the possibility of multiple assertions in that context, as long as they don't halt execution when they fail.

5.1.1 Hard vs. Soft Assertions

Hard assertions halt test execution on failure. Bug found! Stop the test.

Soft assertions let the test fail, but record the result and continue test execution. This means you always get complete test results without halting. That's an ideal separation of concerns. Other benefits of non-halting assertions are better test coverage, stability, and code reuse.

Test code reuse is easier if assertions don't halt execution. You could string tests together for any kind of workflow automation without modifying the code. This makes *end-to-end* testing easier and more robust.

Most test frameworks already implement soft assertions, you'll need to talk to your team and learn if your technology stack can support this kind of testing. If not, the next best thing is limiting each test to one target state.

Let's say you want to modify an automated test to adapt to a new workflow, or share with another team.

When you start to reuse test code, the first thing you'll do is nullify assertions to prevent halting execution. If your tests are built with soft assertions, this is not necessary. More to the point, soft assertions will still tell you where the automation is acting unexpectedly, without breaking it. There is really no downside.

5.1.2 Unit Tests

Unit testing has less opportunities for code reuse, it's true. A unit test ideally is a highly targeted, small, independent single-purpose test.

Usually, your target state will be simple, and a lone assert does the job. In that case, a soft assert will accomplish the same function as a halting assert.

If you are using soft asserts for integration and functional tests, it's worth unifying all asserts to soft assertions for consistency and utility. Consistent code standards are important and contribute to developer adoption.

5.2 Shift Left: Reuse Tests Every Step of the Lifecycle

Shift Left is a trend in the software industry to give more of the testing work to engineering teams directly. A blending of QA team work closer to the development stage. In this book, we've been shamelessly evangelizing this concept from the beginning. Test early, test often.

I would encourage you to push testing even further up the process to planning and really even into product development, emphasizing that QA should be a continuous priority across the entire software development lifecycle and throughout the entire organization.

Of course I'm not just talking about automated tests here, but also specifications. Specs describe functionality which can be used to inform the creation of new specifications in the earliest stages of product development.

Your development phase is where automated testing really shows extraordinary return on investment. We touched on this in Chapter 2. Software development should incorporate unit tests at the very least, run early and often to detect side effects from the new code.

Shift Left philosophy is about running tests early, yes. But the work that comes to support those early test runs include infrastructure and developer operations. The *Shift* represents engineering teams engaging with, or fully taking ownership of that work. To a busy, wary engineer that can look like a lot of extra work that might already be assigned to a dedicated DevOps or QA engineering team. A Shift Left mandate can cause some friction, and you should plan to facilitate that transition of responsibility with clear communication of goals and offer the support you're going to provide for these efforts. For engineers, time is precious. Let them know if you assign them more work you will carve time out for the new work.

One common practice is to prevent new code from being merged into the main version control repository until it passes a suite of tests. Someone will have to set up the rules and functionality for all that, including emergency exceptions where testing needs to be bypassed.

If your software development lifecycle mostly has quality assurance and testing at the end of the process, start shifting left with testing in and around the development phase. Empower your engineering team to build tests and the tools to run them. It will make their jobs ultimately much easier, finding bugs before they commit their work, but it will introduce some new process hoops to jump through.

The upside is most engineers recognize the testing process as a best practice. If a Shift Left represents a major culture change to your team, you may be surprised by the acceptance or even enthusiasm. "Finally, we're getting serious about Quality." and "This will look good on my resume!" Or perhaps even the bitter-sweet yet satisfying "We should have done this years ago."

5.3 Reuse Tests Everywhere

Tests can be reused all over the place!

On our tour of the software development lifecycle in Chapter 2, it's clear we can reuse automated tests in different stages, such as development and staging.

I want you to get outside your comfort zone and consider sharing test code with other parts of your organization. They will love you for it.

The test code your engineering team produces is valuable to other people in your organization, as well as the test plans and behavior specifications you should be writing for each feature. Bringing any one scenario into the necessary target state and then also passing or failing a test scenario.

Sharing tests, test code, and specifications is much easier the more flexible your tests are. By that, I mean if you can separate the target state setup from the assertion in each test. Some people will benefit from both, and many only want to get their software in a particular target state. This is much more difficult when multiple assertions are scattered in any one test.

Let's consider different roles and the benefits of testing they can make use of.

Product Team: Target State

Your product team is going to need to check your work when development is done. Imagine if they could run your automated test, not to simply see a pass/fail but to step through the new work as the target state is set up, and they could verify the results with full functionality.

Support: Target State and Test Results

Your support team is fielding user complaints all day long. They engage the customer directly, note the complaint, and document it. Often, they will also need to reproduce and confirm the complaint, by stepping through the system state in a staging environment to test the wild theories of your users.

Support is an incredibly valuable pool of domain expertise, and many of these people will know your software inside and out. They help find and confirm bugs reported from customers. They can absolutely benefit from your automated tests, quickly confirm part of the system is broken, or load the target system state and study further.

Engineering: Target State, Test Results, and Test Code

If you're lucky, there might be other engineering teams besides yours at your organization. They can all share code to some degree, and if you're not already working together closely, here's a good opportunity. Even if your team is writing tests another team isn't particularly interested in, you're both *running* tests and building test infrastructure. You have something to learn from each other, I promise.

Sales: Target State

One of my earliest code jobs was writing semiautomated sales demonstrations. I would take an existing application and write some automation to put them into a specific state so the sales representative could show that state to a client in person. It was surprisingly challenging, and this was one of the projects that got me interested in automation. It won't take much to build a system like this from your existing test code. You can win major points with the sales team if they need this kind of capability.

Clients: Ask Them!

If you have clients who review your work before it ships, they can use your tests or test plans or specifications, depending on their abilities. Some clients overestimate their abilities, so beware.

Sharing code with clients can be tricky—you might need a security review or legal review before doing so. As mentioned earlier, test code (especially unit test code) closely describes your actual code, which might be a trade secret or otherwise on lockdown.

And, there's a big risk of sharing test code, and then being on the hook so to speak, to support and maintain that code in *their* environment which may or may not be a long-term support recurring nightmare. So beware.

Now that we're all sufficiently wary, share your tests! It can severely cut down client review schedules. For example, some clients or third-party auditors will be conducting user acceptance testing on your software. Sharing some strategic parts of your testing, specifically test plans and specifications, can make that work much faster and easier. With the above cautions still in mind. Specifications are abstract enough to encourage sharing, and that's exactly what they are designed to do.

If a client is doing an integration with your system, writing software to interact with your software, they can absolutely benefit from your behavior specifications or even test code. In this scenario, you're probably providing an application programming interface specification to them formally already. Ask if they need testing resources as well. There's no reason for every party to be reinventing the wheel when you've already defined the system behavior.

5.4 Fixtures, Personas, and Test Data

Your tests will need to use some test data.

It may be encapsulated in the test code, at least at first. Eventually common patterns emerge and you start to notice it would be efficient to share the same data with other tests. The usual indication is when some setup is required external to the test, like preparing a list of parameters to fit more than one test case. Lower-level unit tests may not share much test data.

As your tests climb the abstraction ladder and become more dependent on other components of your system, this will be more and more common.

In some ways, test data starts to outline the target state of a test that needs it. If you need the system in a particular target state, that state is usually represented in whole or part by the data it's working with.

Often what you need is a fake example of a user who is in a particular state. Dealing with users and the data objects that represent them is ubiquitous for most business applications. There are of course many non-user parts of every system. But even the user-unrelated functions of most applications will still need an authenticated user to reach the target state for testing. If you deal with users frequently, your test data will begin to fall into categories of users. The normal happy, valid user. The deactivated user. The special case user.

5.4.1 Personas

Test users can be typified into *personas* to make it easy to share test data that's been configured for a frequently used test case.

A set of personas can be entirely conceptual, not even necessarily digitized, to represent a test case user.

> QA Engineer: Oh yes, you remember our test user
> Mary Doe, with the two kids and normal credit
> history?

You may already be doing this or similar with your test data.

Any test user is a kind of test data that serves a specific purpose, sometimes called a *fixture*.

5.4.2 Fixtures

A test fixture is an older term derived from hardware and electronics testing. In the context of software testing, it tends to refer to test data in general, but the entire testing apparatus is sometimes implied.

The fix in fixture refers to a set of testing tools that are set and predictable.

5.4.3 Test Data as a Service

When your tests mature and stack up, covering more of your application, you'll also notice the accumulation of test data. It can be helpful to organize and separate out the test user cases into *personas*.

Eventually, you'll have to take a look at your test data requirements. Just how abstract is your test data getting in your test code? It may make sense to think about a secure, internal test data provider service.

Providing test data via API could be ideal if you have multiple teams or applications sharing the same test data, or test code. This is an almost required setup to support a microservices architecture.

Some things to keep in mind: Your test data API should be access-protected and secure. Only trusted members of your organization should be granted access. That means you'll need to design it with access control and security in mind.

Remember that test data is closely related to setting up any test specification.

If you decide to build a test data API service, share it! Build a front-end user interface for the less-technical individuals in your organization. All the same benefits of automation reuse apply to test data, and in fact, they are closely related.

5.5 End-to-End Testing and Workflows

End-to-end testing refers to a full workflow for a business use case. That means the test steps are defined from the perspective of a user. A perfect fit for specification: Given, When, Then format is made to address this very application.

Login, logout. Login, do some work, save the work. Login, immediately find the Help button and submit a complaint. You know, the most important workflows.

Priority of which end-to-end tests are needed will likely be set by the business value of the workflow. These can be large, slow, meandering tests and should be considered carefully before building.

High-level tests like this are complex. The related code that comprises even a simple workflow can be thousands of lines, and therefore, hundreds of unit tests would need to be collated to run through the same functionality. Organizing all that from the unit test level is unrealistic.

End-to-end tests are a concept brought over from user acceptance testing, where manual testing from the context of a user is the norm. They can be automated of course—just know they are essentially a string of tests put together to represent a full workflow. If you're writing good Given, When, Then test steps, your tests are already human-readable in a way the Java function they represent is not, to the casual tester.

The closer to the perspective of an end user you get (working with the user interface directly as a user would), the more complexity ramps up. As with all code, complexity increases scope to build and maintenance cost going forward.

The rule of thumb is you should have a solid foundation of unit tests, these are (in theory) the least complex, simplest, and fastest to build and execute. Next is *integration* tests—in short, these are tests that evaluate interactions between one or more systems or components. More complex than unit tests, and they sometimes have external dependencies. At the top of the complexity hierarchy is *functional* or *user interface* testing. These tests run from the perspective of a user, testing from the user interface, but they may be heavily automated to the point of quickness a human can only interpret the end results. Picture a robot furiously clicking and typing at superhuman speed.

End-to-end tests are a concatenation of *functional/user interface* tests, and so they are truly at the top of the complexity mountain. For this reason, consider limited focused effort to build these types of tests in code.

They are also the most clearly useful to a nontechnical observer! Watching an automated workflow happen in real time is a magical experience. Demonstrating these kinds of automated workflow tests can be a great way to show the value of testing to less-technical or test-unaware individuals.

Specification and end-to-end tests are made for each other. A specification that describes a workflow completely also serves as a test plan and a source of system documentation all in one. Specification is minimally complex, and so you don't need to limit effort like you do code. Behavior specifications for full workflows are a good investment. Even better if you can pull together other discrete specifications, reusing code and minimizing effort.

5.6 Specification Reuse

We mentioned the portability constraints of assertions in code, and in the previous chapter, we talked about how Given, When, Then definitions can represent assertions that impede code reuse.

You don't need all those extra And statements. And really if you see a user story with ten steps, take a closer look—they are probably overloaded and should be separate specifications.

Also I mentioned briefly the utility of specification for manual testing. If you're doing any manual testing, and let's be vulnerable for a moment and admit it, there's probably some happening. A specification is a test plan that works just as well for manual testing as automated. Any member of the team can pick up a specification for a manual testing effort, along any point in the software development lifecycle. Even software engineers or people who normally automate all testing. Why would they need a manual backup? Because tests break, and when a test is broken, it represents either a faulty test or a real bug. Either way, someone is going to have to triage the bug, find the code in question, and either fix it or fix the test, maybe both. While this elegant dance commences, with a sensible amount of dramatic vows, curses, and tears, time passes. How much time? Depends on the code fix and complexity of the bug. The point I want to emphasize is this time where a bug is being worked on, the test that caught it is temporarily disabled. Until that test is back online, if you have a good specification, and you have a manual testing backup plan, it's literally a test plan, already written.

Specifications define a test plan, but at the more basic level, they describe system behavior. Earlier in the chapter, we talked about sharing test code with everyone in the organization, and your specifications are no exception. They can help anyone reach a system target state for testing, review, or demonstration. They are a source of truth, living documentation on how your product should behave in each scenario.

5.7 Image Comparison Testing

Visual comparison testing gathers screenshots of your application for analysis and compares them from different environments, different builds, or whatever difference you care to define. It can greatly leverage repurposed test code, if your test code is portable enough.

Consider the problem of assertions halting your test on an error. For a visual test like this, you will want the test to plow through an entire workflow without stopping, no matter what! Don't hit the brakes until we're at our destination. In fact, we should entirely cut the brakes... er I mean disable hard assertions. From there, we can leverage any existing UI test code to step through the site and, with modest modifications, grab our screenshots for comparison.

There are also many services out there you can pay for. If you go this route, have an expert do some research to confirm each product can use your existing test code, or you'll lose one of the main benefits of this type of testing. You may even get stuck writing entirely new test code that only works with their proprietary system, the longer-term effects of which will be an impediment to migrate off that system in the future, lest you lose all that code. Don't get me wrong, writing your own project from scratch isn't for everyone, but if you have portable test code, I think you'll be surprised how much return on investment you can generate relatively quickly, through code reuse.

Before you build it or buy it, ask yourself what goals are being met by visual comparison testing. For my use case, we had clients who wanted pixel perfect design elements and a guarantee that design wouldn't change at all between updates. Importantly, they were willing to pay for it.

There's a hidden cost you should know about this type of testing, file handling and review effort for the results.

Picture a simple website workflow:

>**Given** a valid user, login to the website
>
>**When** the user is logged in and sees the landing page
>
>**Then** logout

This time we take screenshots along the way.

Each screenshot needs something to compare to, so we run the same test case on a different version of the software running on another environment. Likely two different staging environments, configured the same, with comparable test data. For each version, we took screenshots of the login form, the landing page, and the post-logout landing page. Three screenshots for each version of our software.

Now we compare the two versions, overlapping the images which calculates and makes an Image Diff file, with any differences highlighted.

Now for our simple three-step scenario, we have nine image files. Note the Diff highlight file won't be created until there is actually a difference detected, or a significant difference according to your set threshold. Let's remain optimistic and say there was only one Diff out of our test run, referencing the changes between two image files.

The engineer who is running the test will need to look over the results and decide what the difference means. Only by examining both examples and the highlighted differences can they determine if it represents a bug, a known approved change, or something else unexpected. They may need to run the test again, or poke around the system at the target state to understand the issue.

Now consider a full set of screenshots across an entire application or website. That's a lot of files. A lot of screens that need attention and possibly a lot of work for the reviewer. You can further complicate things by archiving one set of screenshots of a particular version to be loaded against future versions, more file handling and more complexity.

All testing requires skilled people to interpret results, triage bugs, and follow up. Visual comparison testing requires more interpretation than average. It's a really cool, visually impressive system, but remember the downsides and consider your testing goals.

5.8 Summary

- Automated testing and test data can have outsized value to any organization, if you know how to use and reuse it.

- When your test breaks, by fail or error, further assertions in that test are never executed.

- Any single assertion depends on one single state of the system under test. I recommend limiting your tests to one single target state per test as a central philosophy.

- Hard assertions halt test execution on failure.

- Soft assertions fail the test, but record the result and yield to continue test execution.

- Most test frameworks already implement soft assertions.

- Unit testing has less opportunities for code reuse.

- Shift Left is a trend to give more of the testing work to engineering teams directly.

- Consider sharing test code with other parts of your organization.

- Test data starts to outline the target state of a test that needs it. Putting the system in a particular target state is usually represented in whole or part by the data it's working with.

- All the same benefits of automation reuse apply to test data.

- End-to-end testing refers to a full workflow for a business use case. Test steps are defined from the perspective of a user. A perfect fit for specification: Given, When, Then format is made to address this very application.

- The related code that comprises even a simple workflow can be thousands of lines, and therefore, hundreds of unit tests would need to be collated to run through the same functionality.

- The rule of thumb is you should have a solid foundation of unit tests, the least complex, simplest, and fastest to build and execute. Next is integration tests—in short, these are tests that evaluate interactions between one or more systems or components. More complex than unit tests, and they sometimes have external dependencies. At the top of the complexity hierarchy is functional or user interface testing.

- End-to-end tests are a concatenation of functional/user interface tests, and therefore the most complex.

- A specification that describes a workflow completely also serves as a test plan and a source of system documentation all in one.

- A specification is a test plan that works just as well for manual testing as automated.

- Specification can help anyone reach a system target state for testing, review, or demonstration.

- Visual comparison testing gathers screenshots of your application for analysis and compares them from different environments, different builds, or whatever difference you care to define.

- All testing requires skilled people to interpret results, triage bugs, and follow up. Visual comparison testing more than average.

CHAPTER 6

Coverage

Code coverage, test coverage, the difference between the two, and what you need to measure each is explained in this chapter. Also covered: managing test value and working with broken tests.

Picture this.

Your team is preparing a big deployment for release. All the hard work of the last month is done and ready for the world. Your principal engineer walks up to you.

"All ready to go, boss."

You contemplate for a moment. "All the merges are in this release branch?" you ask. He nods affirmatively.

You know that no engineer can commit new code without passing a battery of automated tests. Once committed, that code then needs to pass more tests before it's allowed to merge into a final branch earmarked for public release. This gives you a high degree of confidence.

"Alright. Build it to internal staging." Your engineer nods and gets to work. Soon, the application is built to an internal staging environment, and you point your QA lead to it. This team will run end-to-end through business critical workflows, but their work is mostly automated—they simply examine the results.

Most tests pass, a few do not, and you take a look at the report. You turn to your QA lead.

"Which scenarios are these?"

© Ross Radford 2024
R. Radford, *Software Testing for Managers*, https://doi.org/10.1007/979-8-8688-0572-1_6

She is ready with a reply. "These three are related to the new login form. It looks okay when I check it manually, but the code changed last week and the tests need to be updated."

You consider the hole left in your test coverage. Your QA lead knows that while the automated tests are updated, the best thing to do is manually check the application using the business critical scenarios you defined with the client months ago in the planning stage.

"So the other twenty login scenarios are working? Those test other login scenarios, but that means the underlying login system is working fine." She agrees.

"What about that one nasty bug from last time that took so long to find?"

She knows the one. "Yep, our test for that is passing—no regression."

"Alright. Build to external staging. Let's get the client on a call and go over it with them."

On the call, your client's team walks through the business critical scenarios that you have largely automated. They work, and you already knew that. You knew that going into this meeting, and your entire team knew it, too, because they run all the tests themselves as they develop new code. Your client is impressed. The light is green.

"Ship it!"

6.1 The Myth of Code Coverage

Every test is focused on a particular part of the software system under test. In order to provide quality assurance, we must measure how much of our system is *covered* by tests. Coverage is usually represented by a percentage.

Like insurance, you can never have perfect coverage, but at some point, you decide you have enough.

Unit testing is the lowest level, closest to the code, literally counting the lines of code that each test is operating on. Because we can measure that somewhat precisely, unit test coverage is measured in a metric called code coverage. How precise is that measure? If a unit test is written well, it will target a "unit" of code, and it's up to every engineer (or their leadership) to define what a "unit" means. A piece of code will typically have some main functionality which is the heart of the code block. Sometimes, there will be a lot of important routines in a very busy block, and that can be totally valid.

There's no perfect way to categorize everything. In fact, when a test is focusing on a code block, it's up to the engineer writing the unit test to find the important code and assert against that. There could be many, hundreds even, lines of code in a unit test that are not relevant for the test. Accessing data, setup of some object structure, objects that need to be faked or *mocked*. This is more work for our engineer. At the end of it all, the unit test should have considered the irrelevant code, found the important parts, and tested them. When the unit test is later run and the results added up, the entire code block will then be counted as *code coverage.*

Not bad. If the test is done right, that's about as good as it gets for unit tests. There are two limitations.

Most importantly, all these low-level unit tests are not meaningfully connected; in fact, the whole goal is to isolate the units. Even perfect *code coverage* tells you nothing about the various parts of your system actually interacting with each other.

Unit tests have the same limitation that all tests have: When your test breaks, coverage is reduced until the test and the underlying code have been triaged, fixed, and verified. Remember, if your tests never break, they never find bugs.

You don't actually want perfect coverage, and relying on code coverage alone is inadequate.

6.2 Test Coverage

Test coverage refers to the total amount of your software that is tested. Instead of counting lines of code, we're counting the separate parts of the system, defined as *test scenarios*, or specifications if you're fancy.

Unit tests are quite specific and measure *code coverage* only.

Test coverage applies to integration and functional testing, where the associated lines of code are so immense as to be irrelevant. A functional test might cover massive sections of the code, and a report of its "code coverage" becomes incomprehensible.

First, we must quantify how many parts of the system need testing. We might build a suite of integration and functional tests, and then run them, but how would we measure how much of the system they cover? The best way is to define each part of the system with specifications, so there is something measurable to test against.

If your software is broken down into features and components, you can easily see how many of those are testable, which parts have tests ready to run, and what's missing.

Realize that in order to measure coverage on integration and functional tests, you will need to define the system behavior that applies to each test. We covered specification in Chapter 4.

6.3 Only Broken Tests Find Bugs

Tests have a purpose, and it's not just self-soothing, mood-enhancing good vibes; but those are nice too.

Tests provide assurance by catching bugs, and to do that, they break. You can have tests that don't break in the traditional sense, such as using soft assertions to send warnings instead of halting the whole test. This is a good thing as we've discussed already, but it's a moot point when we consider the effects on coverage.

When a test fails, it represents work that needs to be done and a loss of coverage until that work is complete.

Perhaps the test is faulty and needs to be fixed. Maybe there's a real bug that needs attention. Either way, the test is out of commission for the time being and no longer providing coverage.

Tests should break! It's what they were made to do.

There are of course exceptions: flaky tests. Flaky is a term for tests that break constantly, prompting a false alarm, genuinely annoying! I find this problem is usually caused by engineers who are new to writing tests, and they self-correct quickly once they notice the effects of a frequently shattering test suite. No one wants to look at the same failing results of the same broken test every time they run it, especially when they're the ones who have to fix it. It's a problem, but not a huge deal. Think of it as part of the learning curve—some flakes will get in there.

Sometimes, a flaky test is called a false positive, but that language is confusing since the broken test is obviously *negative* and a test that *misses* a bug is more of a false-positive result. I don't actually want to engage that semantic battle, so let's move on. Mitigate flaky tests by refactoring them!

There are more worrisome things than tests breaking too often.

6.4 Tests That Never Break

Perennially, green tests should be a red flag.

What is that test doing if it never breaks? It's not finding bugs. Can it truly then provide assurance? The question may be: Why isn't it ever failing? However, the more salient question is: Are there any bugs this test misses? To determine that, you'll need to look at bugs that are slipping through your testing apparatus, triage them, and locate which system is responsible and which tests should be covering it.

Another possibility is that the test is covering a very stable part of the system. That can happen, and it's a good thing. As testing becomes more ingrained in your development culture from top to bottom, and the effects start to show in the quality of your software, bugs will become less common.

As a software leader, you know that all that testing has a cost, new code, and maintenance. A solid test that never seems to break might not be a problem, assuming it's not missing bugs, but in this case, you still want to take a look and see if the test is frequently updated, indicating maintenance. If the system under that test is so stable it rarely breaks, reconsider all that test maintenance and maybe simplify that test code.

The bottom line is that tests exist to find bugs. If your test result dashboard is mostly green check marks, no bugs should be getting through. Are bugs still getting through?

6.5 Skip, Ignore, and Pay Attention

Broken tests are more or less in maintenance mode until addressed, and they can't provide coverage. When this happens, you need to disable the test, so it's not run in whole or part every time your team runs the test suite. We know it's broken, so turn it off until it's fixed again. This is where to use the *ignore* concept. If you don't ignore the test, people will ignore the repeated failures, and they will fade into background noise.

Ignored tests need attention. They could be broken waiting for a fix, or to be determined, or require some other maintenance like a version upgrade.

Skipped tests on the other hand are intentionally passed over even though they are known to work just fine. And, importantly they are still counted in coverage totals unless you opt out of that calculation. But wait, we want to test everything all the time? Why would we do that!?

Remember all the different environments in the software development lifecycle. Some places you don't want to run every single test. For example, if you are preventing your engineers from merging code into a certain repository until they pass a test suite, you probably don't want to run every single functional or end-to-end test you have—that might take several minutes (or hours!) and that is a lot of downtime for an engineer who is trying desperately to contribute. Maybe you want to limit that testing gate to unit tests, or some select integration and functional testing, and the rest you'll mark as *skipped*.

In order to make good decisions about which tests to skip, you'll need to balance the value of the test against the drawbacks: mainly run time, but also the need for precision in locating reported bugs in code.

6.6 A Better Metric: ERA Model

In this chapter, we've covered coverage in the way it's most used in the software industry.

When tests are run, a coverage total will be produced. Counting up the unit tests and how much code they cover. A separate count of your integration and functional tests, hopefully represented by specifications, the end total being a count of runnable tests vs. specifications.

Did you notice that to get that coverage total, we need to actually *run* the tests?

Standard coverage attempts to quantify how completely a system is tested. Coverage metrics like code coverage can only prove a test is ever actually run against a particular version of the code it covers in the environment it ran in and offers no assurance the test is a good one, simply that it exists.

A test is itself a system, and that system's quality should be continually evaluated, its usefulness justified.

We can do better. I have an advanced model for measuring coverage that can compute all your testing effort down to a simple ratio, a number you can use to make high-level decisions easily with a much more precise level of detail. Fair warning, it takes some effort to understand and apply. If you don't already have a system-wide testing suite in current operation, you must start there first.

Build your tests at every level, get good at it, measure your standard coverage, and then come back here when you want to take your coverage metrics to a higher standard.

Requirements:

- Automated tests working across your software system.

- All appropriate non-unit tests specified as test scenarios or specifications.

When tests are run, a coverage total will be produced.

It begs the question, which environment are we running the tests in and therefore calculating coverage? Does it matter? Yes.

Environment and Risk Aware

or

ERA Test Coverage

ERA has three principles:

- Undefined behavior is not testable and cannot count as coverage.

- Tests that are never run should not be counted as coverage.

- When a bug is found that a test should have caught, note that test as ignored[1] and redesign it.

---

[1] Failed, broken, ignored, or skipped tests do not count as ERA coverage.

ERA principles improve test quality.

ERA *coverage score* measures how many tests were run, when and where, and how many were not.

6.6.1 Score

The ERA coverage score is a ratio.

Passing : possible

Passing = (executed tests – (fail+broken+ignored+
skipped))

Possible = (defined scenarios – skipped)

The ERA score shows a percentage of passing tests on any given environment, for a particular version of the system under test, at any given time.

To represent the score as a percentage, simply divide passing by possible and multiply by 100.

Adding the ratios across all environments provides a comprehensive lifecycle test coverage score as a single percentage.

Software Development Lifecycle with ERA scores

Planning	⇨	Development	⇨	Staging Internal	⇨	Staging External	⇨	Production
754 : 1000		478 : 800		650 : 1000		467 : 820		95 : 100

The software development lifecycle is a stepped process with continuous deployment across nodes, internal and external. Testing should match the cadence of a software system version on its way through the pipeline.

6.6.2 Nodes vs. Versions

In order to prove that a test ran somewhere in the software development lifecycle, you must record when and where it ran.

If a version (say a branch of code) is a static codebase across development pipeline nodes, one coverage score for that version would suffice; but this is rarely the case in practice. Patches, bug fixes, hotfixes, dependency churn, and out-of-sync code make each version a mutating target, changing between environments.

Only by tracking test execution per environment can you see where to improve coverage across the lifecycle.

Some tests need to be skipped in certain environments. An engineer testing locally during development might avoid functional tests that run slowly.

Automated test code should not be deployed to production. However, UAT testing may very well be done in production environments. With ERA, you can measure coverage in all environments comprehensively.

6.6.3 Risk

The direct risk of writing test code is poor/low assurance tests.

The ERA test score exposes unused test scenarios and shows the real effect these risks have on coverage.

6.6.4 Risk Factors

- Quality—Does the test catch real bugs?

- Maintenance—Standard technical debt; someone has to routinely update the tests and decide which tests should be run, and when.

- Execution frequency—How often tests are run.

- Reusability/portability—Code or scenario reuse across environment or platform.

- Performance cost (execution time)—Slow tests are run less frequently.

These factors contribute to reduced coverage.

6.6.5 How To

Measuring an ERA coverage score is easy. Every time you run tests, manual or automated, record the result, context (version and environment) where it ran.

Compare the passing tests to all defined test scenarios in that context to get the score.

6.6.6 Don't Forget

Track your test maintenance. Outside the scope of measuring coverage, this is an important risk to understand. ERA coverage scores will help clarify how many of your tests are in a broken state at any point in time.

6.7 Summary

- In order to provide quality assurance, we must measure how much of our system is covered by tests.

- Coverage is usually represented by a percentage.

- Perfect coverage is not realistic, and not a goal.

- Unit test coverage is measured in a metric called code coverage.

- Code coverage tells you nothing about the various parts of your system actually interacting with each other.

- Unit tests have the same limitation that all tests have: When your test breaks, coverage is reduced until the test and the underlying code have been triaged, fixed, and verified.

- Test coverage refers to the total amount of your software that is tested.

- Test coverage applies to integration and functional testing, where the associated lines of code are so immense as to be irrelevant.

- In order to measure coverage on integration and functional tests, you will need to define the system behavior that applies to each test.

- Flakey tests are tests that break constantly, prompting a false alarm. Mitigate flakey tests by refactoring them.

- Be suspicious of tests that never break.

- Ignored tests need attention. They could be broken waiting for a fix, or to be determined, or require some other maintenance like a version upgrade.

- Skipped tests are intentionally passed over even though they work just fine.

- Environment and Risk Aware (ERA) coverage is an advanced coverage score to improve test quality and calculate test coverage per environment. ERA coverage scores will help clarify how many of your tests are in a broken state at any point in time.

CHAPTER 7

Security

This chapter provides an overview of security testing, terminology, and strategy. Security is a deep, important subject, and this guide is merely an introduction with tips to get started testing. Always enlist the help of security experts where critical systems are at risk.

7.1 Low Hanging Fruit: Static Code Analysis

I was interviewed recently for a podcast, and they asked me a fun question: What was the most surprising bug you've encountered?

I gave two answers because I'm extra. The first was a satisfying tour of a complex technical scenario that reinforces my perceived expertise as a testing expert. All true, but not surprising when you get down to it.

The true most shocking bug I've seen was the first time running a static code analysis evaluation on our codebase and finding an internal password inline in plaintext. I almost spit out my coffee.

Less shocking is helping a friend with a small business and seeing their passwords were things like **123456789**. I'm not joking (but that is a great Mel Brooks joke), I've seen it in the wild.

Did you know you can quickly check your code base for super basic mistakes like passwords or other sensitive information left directly in the code? You can and should.

Static code analysis is static (not moving or changing) in that it isn't trying to run your code. It's really a syntax aware text search through your code to look for common mistakes and risky patterns.

R. Radford, *Software Testing for Managers*, https://doi.org/10.1007/979-8-8688-0572-1_7

It's quite simple in concept and pretty easy to operate. You can easily run it during development if that seems helpful to anticipate new issues as they arise. Before that, if you're starting this type of testing for the first time, you should get ready for a long list of possible bugs to address the first time you run it. Address all that first in a separate effort before you try to make this testing a regular part of your development process.

Static code analysis is interesting because it will flag risky patterns that may be perfectly fine in the context they live in. Rather than a false positive (negative?), you get a whole lot of *maybes*. Someone who knows what they're looking for will have to sort through all those vague threats, and there's a hierarchy of more to less certain risks as a priority guide.

Before you use static code analysis, you should exclude a lot of files, notably your other test code. Test code will throw all kinds of alarms in a Static Analysis, and you aren't shipping that code out to production, so you should exclude it.

Wait, you're not shipping test code out to production right? Right??

In fact, there are a lot of files you should not be sending out to production, and static code analysis will make you very aware of that fact, which is good. Configuration files with passwords, API keys and other credentials stored in them, deprecated or unlinked parts of your codebase, and any kind of test data or fixture files.

When you send your code off to that big cloud in the ether, deployment, you should have a filter (this could be a shell script or similar) that pulls out all the sensitive material, like your test code. You can then use that same filter to pass your code to the static code analysis application long before you ship to production. Win–win.

7.2 Check the Manifest: Software Composition Analysis

You might be wondering, what about all the third-party dependencies our software pulls down when we build it? Is our static code analysis looking at all those extra libraries and packages? Nope. It's looking at the *manifest*. The list of vendors, repositories, and version numbers for each package.

The ratio of third-party software to your original code is absurdly high. If you're building modern software, you're including an absolutely *huge* amount of other code. We're all standing on the shoulders of giants.

> As long as I have you here: Most of those software packages are open source and live on tenacity and scant donations. Consider a tax-deductible donation program at your organization to help the open source engineers who literally build the foundation of your product. There are plenty of ways to contribute. Your team can contribute back code! If you fix a bug, send it back up the chain to help someone else.

All that other code your projects rely on is too big to practically scan for bugs, and as we learned in Chapter 4, it's already being tested anyway. Third-party software, especially the more popular packages, are tested by version by yet other groups for security issues. When your static code analysis test runs a software composition analysis scan, it reads your manifest and looks up the version numbers on each package for existing security issues.

It may seem the best solution is to stay up to date with all the latest versions of every third-party package, but that's not always the case. Many large projects such as programming languages themselves will have newer versions and older versions that get all the latest security updates. These long-term support packages are made to prevent unknown vulnerabilities by halting development of new features, but still providing support and bug fixes for that older version. This can greatly increase stability and security at the expense of new innovative features.

Not all security issues found are critical, and after a scan severity level should be indicated. You will need to decide if the reported security issue is important enough to spend time and energy upgrading that package to a newer version. Sometimes there is no fix yet, and you'll just have to wait! In that case, if the severity is high enough, you may need to try an alternate repository or vendor or regress to a long-term support version. If you have the means, you could fork the project and fix it yourself and even send the fix back up to the original repository. This is the circle of life for open source code.

This composition scanning task can be daunting, and you'll need at least some members of your team to take on the role of Security Compliance Specialist to make these decisions.

Static code analysis and software composition analysis are something you can absolutely take advantage of on your team immediately. There are many other types of security testing, and not all of them are recommended or even possible to take on yourself.

Your organization does need to set policy at the highest levels of what kind of risk is acceptable and what is not. If navigating that question itself seems tricky, you need to hire an expert consultant or maybe even a full-time employee, but either way you will almost certainly need to hire some outside security auditing services.

7.3 You Need Help: Auditing Services

When testing for bugs, it makes sense to test against what we know is expected behavior, and that includes error states. For example, if we try to submit a payment with an expired credit card, we should expect the payment processor to return an error.

ERROR - We're not mad, just disappointed :(

We knew that error was a possibility, so it's the expected behavior of the system and should be defined in a specification.

Recall our discussion in Chapter 4, where there is a whole world of unknown behavior that is so large a possible category we can't test against it in the practical sense.

In the security realm, testing must be more aggressive. To quantify risk of security breach, specialist organizations will in fact test all the unknowns, to the best of their ability anyway.

They (not you, unless you're a security auditing company) should be categorizing all known security vulnerabilities, extrapolating those known attack techniques and strategies to new exploratory testing efforts. These organizations can check your system extensively for vulnerabilities, and they are more qualified to do so than any single hacking enthusiast at your organization. I don't care how cool and smart that person seems.

When you complete a security audit, you're in the same predicament as after a static code analysis test. A possibly long list of issues you'll need to sort out, the whole span from critical to banal but your team will need to decide what is actionable, and your organization should guide them with clear policy, and I'll reiterate, defer to the experts.

7.4 Once Again, the Government: Compliance and Data Breach

All this security stuff is tedious! Wake me up when the PCI compliance audit is over. When does it get exciting?

A data breach!

That's what happens when your company is lax and gets hacked, and your sensitive data is stolen. Possibly held for ransom. This could severely damage your organization and reputation, if not completely destroy it. On a more personal level, employee records including yours could be stolen, and wouldn't that be unpleasant.

It's extremely common and a very real threat to any organization. Make no mistake—everyone is potentially vulnerable to a data breach, no matter how much money and effort they spend trying to mitigate it.

A data breach can open you up to lawsuits, government fines, and of course angry mobs on social media. I'll let you decide which is worse.

If you're working for any government agency or with their data, you will probably have formal audits to ensure your software is relatively secure. If you're processing consumer payment data, you'll get PCI audits. If it's healthcare data, HIPAA compliance.

The process is similar to all testing. They test, you get a report of problems, then you have to triage and fix them or plead your case that a particular issue isn't important. Good luck. But you can test it yourself to be prepared too!

All compliance criteria are based on formalized protocol and generally available to learn and test on your own. If you need to do this kind of testing, bring it into your testing process, gradually at first if it's new territory. Just because you have a scheduled audit doesn't mean you can't be prepared for it. Anticipate, and save everyone some time.

7.5 Data Storage

Secure data storage and data reliability are separate topics, but closely related.

One underlooked technique to secure sensitive data is to avoid storing data you don't need. Maybe you need a name and address of your users, but do you really need their social security number? If you don't have a real business need for it, limit your potential liability and stop keeping that sensitive information.

To store your data securely, you need to encrypt it. In the event of a data breach, the data itself should be locked from view even if access to it is compromised.

The best way to test for encrypted data is a security audit from an expert. Setting up encryption for each record added to your data store will be a software system, most likely third-party provided. An auditor will need to confirm all that is working as intended, but you probably won't be writing automated tests to check that third-party system yourself.

Software composition analysis is more important to tell you about security issues in your data management system toolchain.

The strength of encryption algorithms you use is a technical decision that may be out of your hands, dictated by security compliance. You need to know your obligations to protect the data you store. If you do end up making decisions about cryptography, defer to an expert to find a solution that is best for your data. The stronger the encryption, the more hassle it will be to encode and decode it, and at some point it becomes overkill depending on your use case.

Data reliability falls more into the realm of what you can control. Are you making backups of your data? Are those backups tested to be sure they work if you need them? Are the backups themselves secure with fully encrypted data, and limited access to them? Where do you store those backups anyway?

You won't be writing automated tests for these systems. You'll most likely be relying on existing software solutions to make data backups, encrypt your data, and report irregularities. If you don't have a dedicated database administrator or DevOps team for this, you'll need to assign someone to keep an eye on your data operations full time.

7.6 Data Transport

Data needs to be securely encrypted when it's being sent in and out of your system.

Similar to data storage, you may not have much say in how secure your data transport is required to be. Compliance with PCI payment requirements may set your obligations, or HIPAA, or NIST, etc. Whatever standard you have to meet, it should be clear what needs to be done.

Sending and receiving data will primarily go through APIs that you control, and so you will be responsible for testing data transport at the code level. Fortunately, encryption for sending data is almost certainly going to rely on third-party libraries, so much of the complexity of implementing encryption algorithms will be out of your hands.

I'm intentionally not naming specific algorithms or cryptography solutions here because they are constantly changing. If you do get to choose the cryptography methods your code uses, beware that you'll need to stay informed about industry trends and major developments in that technology domain.

You should be testing your code for proper integration with whatever secure data transport libraries you are using, but again this is security testing and you should rely on the experts. Focused security and compliance audits are the best practice.

7.7 Access: Principle of Least Privilege

The principle of least privilege applies to all individuals in your organization, every last one. You might be the boss, but that doesn't mean you need root access to the production database server.

Social engineering crimes frequently exploit loose access rules. In that scenario, an attacker will trick some random individual into disclosing their credentials to your system, and then the attacker will have the same access as that individual, which hopefully is constrained to their scope of responsibility, but of course may not be.

One challenge with this policy is that roles change. When an individual needs access to a new system they are switching to, it's granted. That facilitation is normal and part of the work process. But when is access removed for old systems an individual no longer needs to work with?

Managing access is important to developer operations, and those operations fall on engineering in whole or in part as well. Security audits will check these levels of access and advise changes if required.

This is an important principle for software architecture as well.

Your users and for that matter your administrators and product configuration agents should only have access to the systems and resources required to do their job and no more.

7.8 Secure Coding Practices

There's a lot to know about secure coding and we're getting into the weeds a bit diving this deep. Still, I want to make you aware of some major topics. Use this as a starting point to learn more and get interested. I'll also briefly cover testing strategy for each.

The principle of least privilege is an important aspect of secure coding practice. This pertains to your users of course, but it may be even more relevant to your application's administrators and configuration agents. Who is allowed to make changes to your product and in what environment? For example, it makes sense to let your engineers access the administration and configuration functions of your product during development and maybe also in staging environments, but probably not in production.

The policy that fits your specific architecture will be unique to your software and may be hard to test for directly. You might consider a test that logs into your product administration function and checks the known access level of that test admin user. You can write a similar test for a normal user of your system.

Sanitizing input means cleaning and filtering raw input submitted by your users. Do you allow your users to set usernames with emojis? If so, best wishes. All input should be sanitized and restricted to only the absolute minimum allowable creativity. When that input is sent to your application from a user interface, it should be checked at that level and then again when it hits your back-end software for processing.

Recall our discussion of fuzzing earlier. Tests here should check that proper input passes the filter. The filter for allowed user input should allow only sparingly and reject *everything else*. We can test the allowed use case, and perhaps a few unallowed cases to trigger an error state, but we do not need to test every possible combination of "everything else."

Prepared statements are a database access pattern where code that works directly with your database is separated out into common reliable functions that should be used instead of manipulating the database directly. A more complex evolution of this concept is a database abstraction layer (DBAL) or object relational map (ORM). These are abstractions that accomplish the same purpose to keep your code from messing with your database unchecked.

Your prepared statements are code that should absolutely have tests written to check the correct function.

Cross-Site Scripting (XSS) is a danger to all web applications and should be top of mind for any web project as a primary vulnerability. Start by learning more about the subject. OWASP.org is a helpful organization that provides guidance on XSS and other security issues.

Static code analysis will make a surprisingly thorough survey of these vulnerabilities in your code. Start with that as a base level test, and zoom into more specific issues as you and your team learn.

Secrets management. Your product probably has one or more central files that store configuration information like API keys and routes, as well as credentials like usernames and passwords for external services.

A better more secure method is to have an external program on each environment server that provides those details when needed, usually at build/compile time. Long story short, they should not be in unencrypted files with the rest of your source code, being passed around to anyone who has access to code. This does create some friction for development, since it's an extra hoop to jump through to set up a local development environment.

Static code analysis will definitely alert you if you have a bunch of credentials stored in files, so that's one way to test. The best solution is to architect your application not to store those values in code in the first place.

Conceptually, this is similar to the problem solved by using a password manager for individual credentials, which you should make available to all members of the organization and encourage them to use it.

7.9 Security Is Social: Team Education

Security is everyone's problem.

As a leader, you are responsible for the security education of your team. So is your top level leadership, so it's likely you have some help at least. Hopefully an organizational mandate to attend online classes or some other method.

All the things you need to know about secure data storage and coding practice are outside the scope of this book, and there's a lot to know. How much your team needs is a decision, how deep to go is another. Hire expert advisors if you need to.

The most common type of security breach is social engineering. You're far more likely to get fooled than hacked. Why would someone bother to pick a lock when they can walk right through the door, with a friendly nod and "Hello!", blending right into the office scenery?

The best way to combat social engineering is education, and your least technical employees are just as much a target as your engineers, if not more so.

This is where credentials like cryptographic keys and passwords should never be reused in multiple places. If a credential or secret is compromised by an attacker, they will try to use it everywhere they can. The larger attack opportunity for that is human input passwords, since humans tend to use passwords they can remember and then reuse those same ones over and over. The solution is to use a secrets manager program to generate and store secure passwords.

7.9.1 Make a Plan

You can build an informative slide deck and give an energetic and passionate presentation on data security, your rapt team in awe over your ability to make such a dry subject interesting and urgent. Everyone claps as you give the final remarks and announce a surprise catered lunch in the break room. Cheers rise through the crowd! Bravo!

Unfortunately, it's not enough. The truth of the matter is you should test each individual team member for the required knowledge, and don't let them off the hook until they pass the test.

If that sounds like too much curriculum to produce yourself, you're correct, it's a lot of important work. It might make more sense to outsource or consult on this one.

It's not just *your* team that needs education. As we've seen, it's truly the concern of every individual at every level. What you need is a security training regimen for everyone, so a flexible system is worth investing in. As in most security topics, it usually makes sense to defer to the experts rather than try to do it yourself. This all ties into the need for a *security standard* for your entire organization. Remember Chapter 3? It's important to have standards. The mandate for security training needs to come from the highest level and include everyone.

Educational material should be specific to the role of each individual. Your engineering department is probably the only one concerned with secure coding practices, for example.

To give you an idea, here's a sample that is by no means comprehensive:

Required training: Complete reading material for each, and complete the quiz at the end to advance to the next topic.

- Social engineering—impersonation, phishing

- Compliance—PCI

- Compliance—GDPR

- Secure coding practices

- Static code analysis

Just because you're a boss doesn't mean you are exempt. Take the training. "We all have to do it" is a great way to demonstrate solidarity.

7.10 Summary

- Static code analysis is a syntax aware text search through your code to look for common mistakes and risky patterns.

- Before you use static code analysis, you should exclude files that will never be deployed to production.

- Software composition analysis checks the dependencies in your project for up-to-date secure versions.

- In the security realm, testing must be more aggressive, but you can't practically do it yourself—hire experts.

- Data breach is extremely common and a very real threat to any organization.

- To store your data securely, you need to encrypt it. In the event of a data breach, the data itself should be locked from view even if access to it is compromised.

- Data needs to be securely encrypted when it's being sent in and out of your system.

- The principle of least privilege applies to all individuals in your organization, and your software should be designed with this principle in mind.

- Sanitizing input means cleaning and filtering raw input submitted by your users.

- Prepared statements are a pattern where code that works directly with your database is separated into common reliable functions instead of manipulating the database directly.

- Cross-Site Scripting (XSS) is a danger to all web applications—learn more at OWASP.com.

- Use a secrets manager in development environments instead of storing credentials in source code files.

- The most common type of security breach is social engineering.

- The best way to combat social engineering is education.

CHAPTER 8

Conclusion

My entire software career has been defined by testing. Testing is always happening, even when it's not the main focus. Every bit of software that runs is tested, first by the developer and then over and over continuously by every single real user. It's such an essential element of software, testing has been a concern even before computers existed!

> *How can one check a large routine in the sense of making sure that it's right? In order that the man who checks may not have too difficult a task, the programmer should make a number of definite assertions which can be checked individually, and from which the correctness of the whole program easily follows.*
>
> —Alan Turing

Alan Turing coined the term *assertion* in reference to computation testing. He was an original pioneer of computer science and greatly influential to this day.

I'll wrap it up with one more quote.

> *Testing shows the presence, not the absence of bugs.*
>
> —Dijkstra (1969)

> *Thanks for reading!*
>
> —Ross Radford

© Ross Radford 2024
R. Radford, *Software Testing for Managers*, https://doi.org/10.1007/979-8-8688-0572-1_8

CHAPTER 9

Pitfalls

No conflicting advice here, just actionable prevention.

Some pitfalls do have lower-priority upsides, indicated with an asterisk (*).

9.1 Coverage*

Coverage measures test availability. It cannot measure results, efficacy, or quality and says nothing of testing frequency. Coverage is useful, but not until you have mastered the basics. Focus on developing a consistent testing process first.

9.2 100% Code Coverage*

Code coverage numbers don't count integration or functional tests, and they shouldn't. Test coverage counts don't show how many tests are broken or in maintenance, and tests will always break. They should. Perfect coverage is an impossible goal. Chasing the long, practically endless tail of this goal is a waste of time. Instead, focus on specifying product behavior and a consistent testing process.

© Ross Radford 2024
R. Radford, *Software Testing for Managers*, https://doi.org/10.1007/979-8-8688-0572-1_9

9.3 Tests That Never Fail

Tests break when they find bugs. Tests that never break should be looked at suspiciously! A test that finds a bug every time you deploy code is far more valuable than one that always passes. If you have tests that frequently break without finding bugs, focus on refactoring those.

9.4 Automation Only*

Manual tests are valuable and are the fallback when your automated tests are broken. If you already have dedicated manual testers, they are domain experts who know your system better than anyone. Automation is great, but don't leave your expert resources in the dust! Focus instead on specifying product behavior. Manual testers are invaluable here.

9.5 100% Automation

Another unattainable goal. Get all your product behavior specified, provable test and code coverage, and security compliance testing, then build a process to do all that for every new feature every time. Then, maybe, worry about automation percentage.

9.6 Screenshots

Gathering screenshots for user interface testing might seem valuable, but the overhead can be significant, and screenshots without context are useless. Not all bugs result in comprehensible visual output, and even the ones that do require reliable steps to reproduce the visual error. In fact, almost all bugs will result in an engineer re-running the test to triage. The file transport, storage, and tracking of screenshots should be done only as needed or to illustrate a specific example. Instead, make your tests easy and painless to run and re-run.

9.7 Xpath vs. CSS Selectors

If you don't recognize these terms, count yourself lucky and move on with your life. There is a minute difference between these two technical details, but they are practically identical. Argument here is a waste of time and should be avoided.

9.8 Fuzzing*

Related to parameterized testing. Algorithms can generate huge testing sets that will generate massive output. Imagine testing every possible character combination in a zip code form field, for example. This is usually overkill. A maximum output of low-priority tests requires a large effort to understand and organize, mostly lost time. Instead, focus on input validation libraries or techniques that are already highly tested and the cases most relevant to your customer base. If none of them are in Iceland, you don't need to test for Hafnarfjarðarkaupstaður.

9.9 Dashboards and Report Data Views*

Before you build these, make sure you know what metrics are important to your team and organization. Beautiful dashboards are satisfying and useful and therefore hard to change once you build them. To reinforce the previous point: if 100% code coverage or automation is your goal, you will forever focus on those numbers and lose sight of real quality. The danger of misdirection is much worse with slick visual charts. Before you build dashboards, learn which metrics you really need to track. If your bosses insist on seeing pretty green dashboards with a 100% test passing rate, ask them why. Refer them to the "Tests That Never Fail" pitfall section.

9.10 Testing Without Specification

If you lack a precise specification of your product's behavior, testing can never be properly organized (except perhaps low-level unit testing). Without a guide of expected behavior, developers have to guess what a test outcome should be for any given feature. This can be a huge time sink for software engineers, with the worst-case result of useless tests. Instead, rely on a proven method to define your product specifications.

Glossary

Software Testing Glossary
Test Types

By relevance

Automated

Software testing that incorporates some amount of automation. All automated processes require human interaction eventually, from interpreting results to maintenance. Not to mention the original time and effort to build it.

Manual

Entering data and working through system behavior as a regular user would. Typically used in contrast to automated tests.

Unit

Refers to the smallest testable unit of code, typically a single code statement or method. Extremely fast to execute.

Integration

Testing interoperability between systems, such as communication between services or APIs. Relatively slower than unit tests but still very fast.

© Ross Radford 2024
R. Radford, *Software Testing for Managers*, https://doi.org/10.1007/979-8-8688-0572-1

Functional

Automated tests that act as a user would, entering data, simulating gestures and clicks, and interacting with the system under test while verifying behavior. Time and resource heavy.

End-to-End

A functional test that comprises an entire workflow. These tests are the most resource and time consuming.

Visual/Image Comparison

A functional test that manipulates system state, captures screenshots, and compares across versions.

Static Code Analysis

Security testing that examines code directly for common known vulnerabilities.

Accessibility

Testing to ensure compliance with government standards for accessibility, such as accommodations for visual impaired users.

Penetration

Security testing employing real-world attempts to exploit the system. Usually handled by specialty firms.

Terminology

Assertion

The point of execution in any test where a pass or fail results.

Automation

Flexible term for any non-manual process.

Behavior

Description of the system under test, specifies a set of system behavior.

Bugs

Unexpected system behavior. The reason we test is to detect and locate bugs.

Coverage: Code

Code coverage means lines of code a unit test evaluates. Lines of code is not a useful metric for other types of tests.

Coverage: Test, Scenario, Feature, Component

Test coverage refers to the scenarios and behavior defined by the testing suite, compared to untested scenarios or use cases.

Continuous Integration

A software development method where changes are continually reintegrated to the system. Highly reliant on automated gated testing.

Exceptions

Unexpected software behavior. Automated tests are also code, and so test execution will result in either pass, fail, or an exception.

Execution, Run

Performing an automated test. All tests are executed on a particular version of the system under test on a particular environment representing a stage of development.

False Positive/Negative

A test resulting in an incorrect failure report. Typically due to mismatched or inadequate system behavior specification, or incorrect test code.

Fixture

Testing data to be used in tests. Should be standardized and shared across your organization. Sometimes called sample.

Fuzzing

Also called parameterized testing. Algorithms can generate huge testing sets that will generate massive output. Imagine testing every possible character combination in a zip code form field. This is usually high effort for low value.

Gated

When code is sent to a repository or automated build process, automated tests can deny the code based on automated test results.

Given, When, Then

A system of simplified language for specifying software behavior. Testing frameworks can then automate the steps in each definition directly.

Manifest

Dependency management systems will have a project specific configuration file listing all the versions of third-party software packages and their repositories. This is a manifest.

Mock/Mocking

Specific to unit testing, in which a test will simulate dependencies to execute the code under test. Sometimes also used to refer to test data/fixtures.

Pass, Fail

Ideal result of any test execution. Other possible results are exception, and intentionally skipped or ignored tests.

Skipped, Ignored

Tests marked as excluded from execution. Test code in need of maintenance or updates should be marked ignored. Tests not relevant to the testing goals for that environment should be marked skipped. The difference is skipped tests are still counted as working for the purpose of calculating test coverage. Ignored tests are not.

Specification

Behavior of the system under test.

System Under Test

Application or other software we subject to tests. Software environments can have many systems; the system under test is our focus.

Test Driven Design

A software development process that encourages tests to be written before other code, which thereby provides a target passing test for the engineer to build toward. Not a recommended practice for all teams.

Test Framework

Most code languages and development stacks have their own native testing tools. There are others not specific to any one language.

Testing Hierarchy

A logical hierarchy diagram suggesting priority of testing effort, with the largest set of unit tests making the foundation, smaller amounts of integration tests in the middle, and finally limited functional tests on top.

Triage

Diagnosis of a new bug, a borrowed medical term. Any bug reported by a failed test must be investigated.

Quality Assurance

QA can refer to the concept of testing, or a dedicated test engineering team. Used to differentiate between normal software engineering and user acceptance testing.

User Acceptance Testing

Testing from the perspective of a user, usually through a graphical user interface. This term usually refers to manual testing, but all manual processes can be augmented with at least some automation.

Index

© Ross Radford 2024
R. Radford, *Software Testing for Managers*, https://doi.org/10.1007/979-8-8688-0572-1

T

www.ingramcontent.com/pod-product-compliance
Lightning Source LLC
LaVergne TN
LVHW051641050326
832903LV00022B/842